TTI Lite

THE TIM🌐THY INITIATIVE

"What you have heard from me in the presence of many witnesses entrust to faithful men who will be able to teach others also."

2 Timothy 2:2

TTI Contact Information: admin@ttionline.org

TTI Website: www.ttionline.org

TTI Lite

An Overview of TTI's Foundational Curriculum

© 2014 by The Timothy Initiative

Scripture quotations are from: The New King James Version

Copyright © 1979, 1980, 1982 by Thomas Nelson, Inc.

Used by permission. All rights reserved.

First Edition-North America

Expectation For Every Disciple Who Makes Disciples:

I, _____ understand that the Timothy Initiative has a goal of training disciples who make disciples and plant churches. I understand that a church can meet in a building, house, or even under a tree. I also understand that a church can consist of 10-15 believers gathered together to worship God.

As a Timothy Initiative disciple maker, I commit myself before God and my mentor, to establish one new church/fellowship within an agreed upon time frame.

I understand that I have been chosen as a disciple maker not only to be trained in the Word of God using TTI material, but also to establish at least one disciple making church.

_____

Signature

_____

Commitment date

STOP!
Do not go any further without signing above!

Table of Contents

Welcome to TTI Lite

The purpose of this training course is to equip (Timothy's & Titus') Disciples who will make Disciples. We expect that by going through this course:

- Learners will be discipled and trained to become church planters.
- Learners will be equipped to share their faith with others.
- The Gospel will be spread at a fast pace.
- Churches will be planted.
- Learners will be equipped and trained in the essentials of the Christian Faith.

If you are studying this book it means you are interested to be a second generation church planter. Your teacher/mentor has likely already planted a church and is now training you to do the same. This training is not limited to you. We expect that you also will train others to be church planters and multiply as well with the tools and principles you learn from this material.

Introduction: What is The Timothy Initiative?

The Timothy Initiative is an international church planting organization. TTI was established with the purpose to train and equip Church Planters. We specifically target church planters who lack the means and/ or availability to receive balanced, Biblical, theological, and practical church planting training throughout the world. Every trained church planter is expected to plant at least one multiplying and reproducing church as well as recruit and train others to do the same. The goal is to start a church that will be a church-planting center.

What is the Mission of TTI?

TTI's mission is to see reproducing, multiplying church planting movements. In partnership with other national movement leaders, TTI desires to penetrate the nations and cultures with the Gospel of Jesus Christ.

What are the Core Values of TTI?

1. **Kingdom Focused:** It's all about The Kingdom, so we share the work and give God the credit.

2. **Spirit-Led—Scripture-Based:** The Holy Spirit and The Holy Scriptures are our guides in planting and multiplying churches.

3. **Integrity First:** God values integrity; so do we.

4. **Disciple Making:** The best way to plant churches is by making disciples.

5. **Prayer is Priority:** First we pray, then we plan and then we plant our churches.

6. **People Matter:** All people matter to God, so we reach out to everyone.

7. **Faith Driven:** We want to bring glory to God; if there is no faith involved, there is no glory for God.

What Is Our Definition of a Church?

For TTI, our working definition of a church is: A group of believers under the authority of Biblically qualified leadership, who meet together regularly to worship the Father, study and communicate the Word of God in the power of the Holy Spirit, pray and fellowship together, observe the ordinances, and go out to share the love of Christ with the lost world. A church can meet in a building, in a house, under a tree, or anywhere! We suggest that every church that is planted have at least three unrelated individuals.

Chapter One
Interpreting and Understanding the Bible

This chapter focuses on **interpreting and understanding the Bible.**

Imagine finding a letter that was written 100 years ago. You do not know who wrote it or why. You do not know the person to whom the letter is written. You do not know the people, places, or even some of the words that it mentions. Now imagine you were asked to explain the letter to another person. You might be able to figure out some things, but you might make some wrong guesses as well. In order to explain the letter correctly, you would need to know more about the authors, recipients, and the purpose of the letter. It would also be helpful to know the background of the author and the recipients.

The Bible is the same. If we do not understand where the Bible came from, how it was written and why, we may make mistakes when trying to interpret and understand the Bible.

The first question we must ask is *"What is the Bible?"* The Bible is God's word written down. It carries the very breath and character of God. It is through these Holy Scriptures that God communicates with us.

Second, we ask, *"How did we get the Bible?"* God revealed Himself to people and told them to write down His words completely and accurately, free from error.

Third, we ask *"Who wrote the Bible?"* God chose 40+ people to communicate His message both orally and in writing. These stories and writings were historically written down, reproduced and shared with others. God combined His message with the words and language of the author to express the things of God. As a result, the Bible is the combination of God's thoughts communicated through human words and understanding. These writings form what we now call the Bible. The Bible is an unchanging set of stories, teachings and principles. There is nothing more to add to it.

How do we know that the Bible is complete?

Jude 3 — This part of the Bible instructs us to *defend the faith that God has entrusted once for all time to His holy people.* This verse disagrees with anyone who tries to claim that God has given them a new revelation. Though the Holy Spirit certainly gives us direction in our lives, the Holy Spirit never adds to or contradicts the Bible.

Instead of preserving the original writings of Scripture, God gave man the responsibility of protecting it, copying it, and translating it.

1. Before there were hand written copies and printing presses, much of Scripture was communicated orally.

2. After some time, these words were written down and reproduced by individuals who copied the writings by hand. They did this as accurately as possible, and the Bible we have today is a result of those copies (see *John. 14:26*).

This shows why it is worthy to be trusted as a guide of our faith. It gives all people the opportunity to hear and read God's Word regardless of their language. **The Bible was the first and most translated book ever in human history!**

Who was the Bible written to?

The Bible was written to all mankind. Through God's Spirit and His Word, He reveals Himself to us. The Bible is God's Word! The purpose and goal of God's communication with us is so we can be in a relationship with and worship Him. When we read, hear, and obey the Word of God this must be our ultimate goal.

Interpreting and understanding the Bible is extremely important because most everything we know about God and Christ comes from His Word. If you do not understand it, or if you interpret it incorrectly, you can mislead yourself as well as those you teach. Also, consider how your culture is different from the cultures in which the Bible was written, so it is your job to interpret Scripture in your context.

One of the primary roles of a disciple who makes disciples is to give proper attention to both the meaning of Scripture and its application in their culture. We pray your disciples will bear spiritual fruit and grow. This chapter will help you on your mission!

The Beginning

The first person introduced in the Bible is God. The first human being mentioned is a man named Adam. He was the first human of God's creation. Created perfect, he lived in a faultless garden named Eden. God said it was not good for this man to be alone, so He created a perfect woman named Eve. Adam and Eve enjoyed the garden, a perfect relationship with each other, and direct communication with God. There was one tree in the garden God told them not to eat from, but Satan, disguised as a serpent, came and deceived them. They ate from the tree, disobeying God's command. Disobedience is sin. This sin broke the relationship they had with God and with each other. They felt fear and shame, so they hid themselves. God, who was their Father and Friend, became their Judge. There was now separation and they no longer had direct access in their relationship with God. (*Genesis 1-3*).

All humans originate from this first man and woman, Adam and Eve. As a result of their sin, all people have a broken relationship with God. In this state we cannot have a proper relationship with God.

Example: On a cloudy day, you cannot see the sun or the moon or the stars above you. They are blocked from your vision. However, when the clouds go away you can see everything that you could not see before. Through the Bible, God reveals Himself to us so that we may see Him. He has chosen to reveal many things to us in the Bible, including His Son, Jesus. Apart from God, we cannot see Him or know His mind. Fortunately, **God provided a way to remake the broken relationship with us!** The way we learn about fixing this relationship is through God's Word. (We call this process revelation).

1. The Problem: We are separated from God and cannot see Him (*Isa. 55:8; 1 Cor. 2:9*).

2. The Goal: To be in proper relationship with God. The way we do this is by knowing Jesus Christ and becoming more like Him. (*Rom 8:28; 2 Cor. 3:18*).

3. The Reason: When we become like Jesus Christ, our lives experience transformation (*1 John 2:6*).

4. The Result: The glory of God is evident in and through our lives (*2 Cor. 3:18; Psa. 96:3*).

Example: Imagine you are walking along the road and you see a man jumping up and down waving his hands in the air. One person might see this man and think "That man needs help." Another person might pass by and think, "That man is drunk." A third person might look at him and say, "That man has been kicked out of the village." There can be as many interpretations of that man's actions as there are people walking down the road. However, we can't know what his behavior really means unless he explains it to us.

The Bible tells us everything we need to know about how God can fix our relationship with Him, through His Son Jesus.

1. Jesus came to earth as a person to reveal God to the world.
2. The Old Testament was the preparation for Jesus, and everything in the New Testament was an explanation of Jesus.

Assignment

Practice telling the story of Adam and Eve. After telling the story answer the following questions:

1. What do we learn about God?
2. What do we learn about Man?
3. What principles do we learn, or what sins should we avoid?
4. What commands are there to obey, or examples to follow?
5. What is my response? What must I do?

Application Points for the week:

By answering these questions you are interpreting and applying the Bible! A simple and easy tool to use when interpreting the Bible is called the SWORD method.

*"The Word of God is living and active, sharper than any **double-edged sword**. It penetrates even to dividing of soul and spirit, joints and marrow; it judges the thoughts and attitudes of the heart." Hebrews 4:12*

Everything we need to know about God and man is revealed in the Bible. The Bible also reveals God's desire for us through examples and commands we should follow. Anyone who wants to know God and follow Jesus must read the Bible and seek to follow its commands.

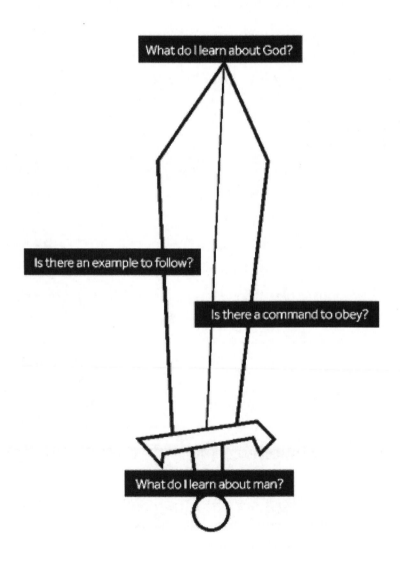

THE SWORD METHOD

What do I learn about God?

Is there an example to follow?

Is there a command to obey?

What do I learn about man?

When the Bible is read, we can learn its meaning by asking these questions based on The Sword Method picture:

The top of the sword points toward God. We ask the question: **What do I learn about God?**

The bottom part of the sword points us toward man. We ask the question: **What do I learn about man?**

The two edges of the sword penetrate our lives, creating change. They lead us to ask the questions: **What principles do we learn, or what sins should we avoid? What commands are there to obey, or examples to follow?**

The side arrows on the handle of the sword direct us to the sections before and after. This is the context, and gives the complete understanding and background of a verse or group of verses. You are not free to use verses however you want.

What else do we learn from this passage?

We now know that God reveals Himself to us through His Word (the Bible) and the Holy Spirit.

1. God's Word:
   - The words, messages and stories in the Bible are God-breathed (inspired and without error) and perfectly accurate.
   - Although men recorded the Bible, its words are the very words of God.
   - The Apostle Paul and all the writers speak, but not with their own wisdom. Instead they reflect the wisdom of God. (*1 Cor. 2:6-15*).

2. Holy Spirit:
   - *1 Cor. 2:6-15* reminds us that to know the mind of God, He must tell us. No one knows the thoughts of God except the Spirit of God.
   - *John 16:7-13*: We generally believe that life would be easier and decisions simpler if Jesus was standing beside us. But even when Jesus was on the earth He said it is good for us to have the Holy Spirit as our Comforter and Guide.

Summary

The main point is that we must know we are helpless apart from God. We cannot know about God without His gracious involvement on our behalf. If we forget this point we can wander towards a religion that emphasizes our own work, ability and intelligence. We must be careful not to do this!

Some Basics of Interpreting the Bible

As a result of God's communication process, we have a miracle book, unlike any book in the world. It is the only one of its kind. It is just as true as God standing in front of you and speaking directly to you. God has protected His Word so that it will guide us in the right direction. Always remember that Scripture interprets Scripture. If you are unclear on one verse or one chapter, look for other verses and chapters on the same subject to compare and contrast. For example, *Luke 8:5* is interpreted by *Luke 8:11-12*.

1. Using the SWORD method of interpreting and understanding the Bible will guide towards proper interpretation.

2. As a result of carefully applying what we learn in the Bible, we develop correct doctrine and correct experience.

   - **Doctrine** that we receive from Scripture is built on the foundation of interpretation.

   - **Experience** grows out of doctrine. This experience or application will be consistent with both Scripture and doctrine.

   - To consider this relationship another way, imagine the process as a house. Interpretation would be the foundation, doctrine would be the building that rests upon interpretation, and experience would be the roof that rests upon doctrine. Consider the house in the space following (or draw one for yourself) and use it to explain this principle to others.

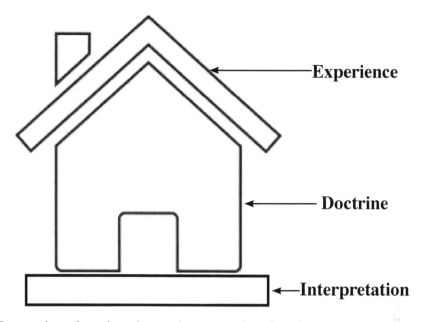

Remember, there is only *one* interpretation, but there are many applications. We must simply make sure our applications grow directly out of correct doctrine, and correct interpretation.

Caution: Be careful not to begin with Experience. A roof makes a poor foundation. Do not reverse the order. Do not work from experience to establish principles, and then develop an interpretation. When you begin with experience, you will not be able to interpret Scripture clearly. The house drawn above is the structure we are seeking to build. Make sure you understand this before moving on!

Why is it important to learn how to interpret the Bible?

Consider the following story:

> *One day there was an Ethiopian returning home from a religious pilgrimage. He read from the book of Isaiah in the Bible but was unable to understand what he was reading. God sent a man named Philip to interpret and explain what he was reading. Philip asked him, "Do you understand what you are reading?" The Ethiopian said, "How can I understand unless someone tells me?" Philip then gave a proper interpretation of the passage. As a result, the Ethiopian put his faith in Christ (For the full story see Acts 8 and Isaiah 53).*

After discussing the story answer the following questions:

1. What do we learn about God?
2. What do we learn about Man?
3. What principles do we learn, or what sins should we avoid?
4. What commands are there to obey, or examples to follow?
5. What is my response? What must I do?

Application Points for the week:

From the story we learn several things.

First of all, seeing words on a page of the Bible does not mean the reader can understand them. **Observing what the Bible says is only the first step of interpretation.**

Secondly, this story reminds us that proper guidance can help someone interpret the Bible. Like the Ethiopian, the meaning of the words is not always easily apparent without direction from another Bible student.

Consider the Biblical background:

1. **The Bible's Unity**: There is great variety in the Bible. The Bible was written in many forms, by many authors, on a variety of subjects over two thousand years. There is a common subject, a common purpose, and no contradictions.
2. **The Bible's Worldview**: The Bible has a God-centered worldview. This means that everything in Scripture views the world through the eyes of God. God gives meaning to all experiences. He determines what man is, what knowledge is, what meaning is and what nature is.

Culture

When reading the Bible it is always important to consider the culture of the author, how your own culture impacts your interpretation, as well as the perspective of the culture that you will communicate the Word of God.

Application

Application is communicating the present-day importance of a Biblical text. Specifically, how that passage may be put into action, and inviting and urging the hearers to do what they understand. It is only through the leading and guiding of the Holy Spirit that we can fully understand and apply the truth of the Bible.

It does little good to know the truths of Scripture yet fail to put them into practice. *James 2:19* tells us that even the demons believe in God! What separates us from them is whether our lives are changed by what we know and obey. **It is not enough to have the right interpretation if that interpretation has no impact on your life or on those around you. Application is ultimately what matters to God. We must take the Truth of God and help others move from understanding to action.**

Assignment

Read the story:

> *Once there was a man on a long journey. On the way he was attacked by thieves, beaten up, and left for dead. Many people passed by, including religious leaders and important people, yet no one cared for him. There was one man though, a foreigner that was not accepted well in that country, who found the man. This foreigner stopped his journey and took care of the bleeding man. He attended to his wounds and needs as well as paid for his expenses to make sure he was brought back to health.* (See *Luke 10:25-37*)

The following questions have been answered as an example of using the SWORD method. Consider the questions and answers below.

1. **What do we learn about God?**

   - God is a merciful God and expects us to show mercy to others in need.

   - God's expectations are not determined by color, caste, tribe, or religion.

- God expects us to love Him and love others as we love ourselves.
- Our love is expected to be shown in our actions not just our words.

2. **What do we learn about Man?**

   - The heart of man is wicked, selfish and lacks compassion.
   - Man does not please God by simply being religious.
   - Man looks to earn favor and salvation by their works or merit.
   - Man has his own standards established him and others.

3. **What principles do we learn, or what sins should we avoid?**

   - Not helping someone in need is actually hurting someone in need.
   - Sins to avoid: stealing, attacking, and taking advantage of others.
   - We should love God and others just as we love ourselves.
   - Care for those in need.

4. **What commands are there to obey, or examples to follow?**

   - Follow the example of the foreigner, considering the needs of others more than your own needs.
   - Jesus said: "*Go and do likewise.*"

5. **What is my response? What must I do? Application Points for the week:**

   - I will love the Lord and others as I love myself and encourage others to do the same. I will show this love by:
   - Evaluating the needs of the community, actively share the Gospel, and showing the love of Christ in word and actions.
     - ▶ Offer food to my neighbor in need.
     - ▶ Offer shelter to the orphan without a home.
     - ▶ Take the sick person in my village to the hospital.
     - ▶ Help the old man of the community in his duties.

What is the Bible?

Answer: It is God's Word, written down. It is the way that He communicates with us.

How did we get the Bible?

Answer: *Inspiration*

The words in the Bible are God breathed...they are completely accurate and free from error.

How was the Bible transmitted?

The Bible was communicated orally... and historically written down and reproduced.

Translation:

Original language into a local language.

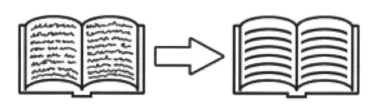

Importance of Application:

You must apply what you've learned. Consider *Luke 10:25-37* as you have already studied this above using the SWORD method.

A Jewish man was attacked by robbers.

Several Jewish religious men passed by, but they offered no help.

An outsider (Samaritan) rescued and cared for the man.

Which of these men was a neighbor to the man who was attacked?

The outsider (Samaritan)

Jesus told them, "Go and do likewise."

Possible applications:

Mercy

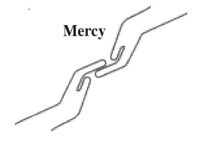

Love others as yourself

Love through actions,
not only words

Do not show prejudice

  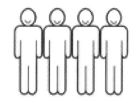

Chapter 2
Sharing the Word of God

The call to make disciples goes out to every follower of Christ. Every believer is a disciple, and every disciple, a disciple maker. One of the most important tools for a disciple who makes disciples is clearly and confidently communicating the Word of God.

Read *2 Timothy 4:1-5* and notice some observations:

1. Communicating the Word of God is very important.
2. We share the Word of God... and His message.
3. We need to be ready and willing at any time.
4. What we share needs to be true.
5. What we share requires commitment.
6. Sharing the Word of God is the work of an evangelist and will be rewarded.

We possess the greatest news ever told to anyone. That's what the word "*Gospel*" means, *Good News!* Let us pray to God to make us faithful communicators of His Word.

God has chosen us to proclaim His Word and communicate His message to others (*Rom. 10:17; John. 15:16*). We must work as hard as we can to be the best communicators of the Gospel, for His glory. Consider the following:

1. How can anyone hear without someone sharing the Word of God? (*Rom. 10:13-15*).
2. How can we communicate in a way that our message is clear and practical? (*Col. 4:2-6*).
3. We must communicate the Bible as it is, to people as they are (*Acts 17:16-34*). We must communicate sensibly to the culture of our listeners.

Example:

One day Paul, one of the leaders in the early church, was traveling through an unfamiliar city named Athens. The people there worshiped many gods and enjoyed discussing and debating religion. As Paul waited for someone in town, he talked with some of the people about their gods. He noted that they worshiped many gods, including an "unknown god." Paul began his message by revealing the unknown God as the Creator of everything. Without condemning them, He presented Jesus Christ as this unknown God; a God in whom they have their purpose and meaning. He also warned them of a coming day where God will judge all men. Some listed to him but others mocked. His message, however, was relevant to the people (See Acts 17:16-34).

Learning to Teach like Jesus

Jesus must be our model for teaching. To capture the attention of men and women like Jesus did, we must communicate spiritual Truth the way He did. There is so much to learn from Jesus' style of communication. Consider the following story:

There was a woman in a village that, because of her lifestyle, was rejected by her own people. One day as she was drawing water at the well, all alone (because her community refused to associate with her), and Jesus approached her. This woman knew Jesus was from a culture that would not interact or associate with her. Jesus, however, asked her to give Him water.

She asked him, "How can you speak to me when you are from a hostile ethnic group?" Jesus replied, "If you knew who I AM, you would have asked Me for living water." She wondered how He could give her this living water. Jesus also revealed that He knew about her lifestyle (that she had five husbands and the man she was currently with was not her husband).

The woman thought that Jesus must have been a prophet. Jesus revealed His true identity, as the Messiah. After this she left her water, returned to her village and told all she had seen and heard. She told those in her village to "Come and see the man who told me all I ever said and did." Many villagers went to see Jesus. Based on the woman's testimony and what they saw and heard from Jesus, many of them placed their faith in Christ. (See *John 4:1-42* for the full story)

1. <u>Jesus began with the woman's needs, pains and interests</u> – Our message to the lost must be good news. You can gain the attention of people by starting with their needs, hurts, and interests (*John 4:1-42*).

2. <u>Jesus related the Truth to real life</u> – His goal was for application because He desires to transform people, not only inform them. **The Bible was not given to increase our knowledge but to change our lives.**

3. <u>Jesus spoke to different people with different styles</u>:

   • He told stories to express his message. Jesus was a master storyteller.

   • Jesus used simple language/terms that normal people could understand.

Assignment

In *John 4*, the woman in the story immediately went and told all those in her village about the Messiah. When she came to believe in Christ, she desired to tell others. You too have a story to tell. You too have met the Messiah and now believe in Christ.

On the next page, write **your story** of how you met Jesus! Then go and share it this week with five new people! Remember to consider the following as you do this:

• **Include the following:** How I lived and what my life was like before I believed in Jesus. How I came to know Jesus (Or how I recommitted or rededicated to an earlier decision). How my life changed after I believed. The ultimate message: "Knowing Jesus as Lord and Savior changed my life!"

My Story

_____

_____

_____

_____

_____

_____

_____

_____

_____

_____

_____

_____

_____

_____

_____

_____

_____

_____

_____

_____

_____

Preparing our minds: Do you understand the passage?

It is very important that we understanding the passage we are communicating to others.

1. The Bible is the ultimate authority, not the teacher. The teacher is under the authority of the Bible.

2. Proper interpretation is the source for effectively teaching the Word of God: The Bible, properly interpreted and clearly taught, is powerful (*Heb. 4:12*).

3. God works through His Word in the hearts of men and women (*Isa. 55:10-11*).

4. There are several ways to help you understand the true meaning of the Scripture:

   • The Holy Spirit helps us understand the Bible (*John 16:13*).

   • Scripture itself interprets Scripture. We learn the meaning of Scripture as we faithfully study the Bible.

   • The Holy Spirit speaks to us through other believers (*Acts 8:26-35*).

   • We learn the meaning of the Bible as we obey the teachings of the Bible (*James 1:22-25*).

5. Remember the role of the Holy Spirit as you prepare and as you teach: **The Holy Spirit takes the Word of God, to reveal the Truth of God, to accomplish the work of God** (*John 16:7-14*). Consider the following saying:

   • "The Scripture without the Spirit dries up." Much like a plant shrivels up if it has no sun or water, so the Holy Spirit is necessary to bring life to the message.

   • "The Spirit without the Scripture burns up" If the focus is on experiences and not based upon the Bible, it is like a wild fire: out of control and damaging.

   • "The Spirit and the Scripture together builds up." When building a house, you use both brick and mortar. You cannot build a strong house without them both. Likewise, you must have both the Spirit and the Scripture in order to build up the church.

6. The Bible is to be read by everyone, with faith, consistently, prayerfully and with Christ as the focus.

- The Old Testament – the Good News is coming.
- The Gospels – the Good News is revealed.
- The Acts – the Good News is spreading.
- The Epistles – the Good News is explained.
- The Revelation – the Good News is fulfilled.

The Role of the Holy Spirit in Communicating the Word of God

1. The Holy Spirit Gives the Ability to Understand God's Truth in the Bible (Eph. 1:17-18).

2. The Holy Spirit Provides Guidance: We must trust God to guide us in our preparation and communication (*John. 14:26*).

3. The Holy Spirit Gives Empowerment: The Holy Spirit fills and empowers us for daily living and service (*Eph. 5:18*). We must rely on Him, praying for Him to empower us, and our message to impact the hearts of others.

4. The Holy Spirit Brings Conviction: The Holy Spirit, not the teacher, convicts listeners of their need for Jesus. He convicts them of their sin, reveals God's righteousness and God's coming judgment (*John. 16:8-11*).

5. The Holy Spirit Brings Transformation: The Spirit of God loves to transform people's lives. The end result of transformation is the fruit of the Spirit (*Gal. 5:22-23*).

Developing and Training Others to Communicate the Word of God

1. *Acts 13:1-3* begins with the Holy Spirit directing the leaders of the Church at Antioch to set apart some men for a missionary journey of church planting. They prayed for them, laid hands on them, and sent them on their way. **Part of your job is to find, develop and train others also.**

2. **Reproducing Yourself**: *2 Tim. 2:2* is a verse that TTI has built its ministry on. The Timothy Initiative is named after this verse.

In this one verse there are four generations of leaders: Paul, Timothy, Faithful Men, Others. Timothy was called to reproduce his life into "faithful men." So the question to you is: *who are you training? As you learn, also expect those you teach to teach others.*

3. **Teach the Word of God: Be ready and willing at any time.** The Word is alive...our Lord is alive...will you be alive and ready to communicate His Word, at all times?

Key words to remember as you share the Scripture:

1. **Truth** - Make sure what you are teaching is what the Scripture actually says. Preach the Word, not opinions.

2. **Clarity** - Speak the Truth of God's Word in such a way that your listeners can understand what you are saying. Speak so that even the young children can grasp what you are saying.

3. **Passion**- Speak in such a way that your listeners can tell you really believe what you are saying. Your message must cause you to respond in obedience and love. Speak as if it is your last time on earth to share the Good News.

4. **Grace** – Remember that everyone is hurting. Everyone is struggling. Make sure as you communicate God's Word you do so with love and compassion for those who are lost and without Christ.

Assignment

Read *John 4* and use the SWORD method. This is the story of the woman at the well. Share a five to ten minute message with your mentor, emphasizing the application of the story. After practicing, ask for a time to share the same message in your leader's church.

How will you train others to share the message and stories you teach them? Hold them accountable to also share the story with others. Write down two names to share with this week.

Communicating the Word of God

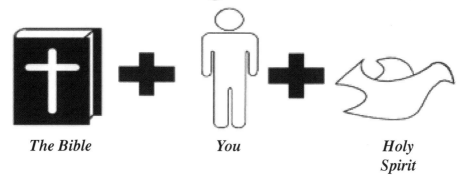

The Bible   *You*   *Holy Spirit*

Leads to...

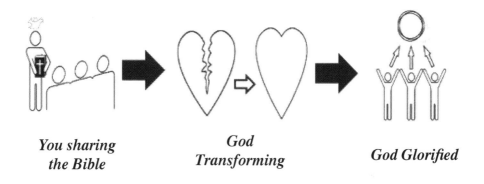

You sharing the Bible   *God Transforming*   *God Glorified*

The Role of the Holy Spirit in Communicating the Bible

For the speaker the Holy Spirit provides:

1. Understanding of God's truth and the Bible
2. Guidance
3. Empowerment

For the listener the Holy Spirit provides:

1. Conviction
2. Transformation

Communicating: When having a conversation, there are several things to remember. Observe how Jesus told this story:

The Story	Jesus	You
A man asked Jesus, "How do I inherit eternal life?"	Answered & asked questions: "What does the law say?"	Engage your audience. Ask and take questions. Choose relavant topics.

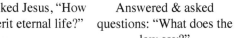  

Man asks for clarification: Law says love God and neighbor. Who is my neighbor?	Answers with a story: A man was robbed and left for dead. Two men ignored him, and one helped.	Use stories to help them understand.

The man understands the story: The man who helped was the neighbor.	Tells him to go and do likewise	Give a call of action to obedience and an application

  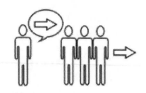

As you communicate the Word of God to others, encourage others to do the same also.

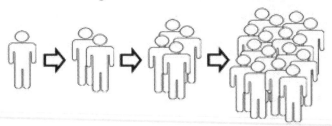

Chapter 3
Church Planting and The Book of Acts

The Great Commission

When you ask most people to open their Bibles to The Great Commission, most of them will refer to *Matthew 28:18-20*. This is only one of at least five times that Jesus gave His disciples the command to go into the entire world and share the Gospel. Let's begin by taking a fresh look at the Great Commission in all five passages.

Assignment

Read the following Great Commission verses and make notes about the unique parts of each book.

John 20:21

Mark 16:15

Matthew 28:18-20

Luke 24:44-49

Acts 1:8

What is a Commission? A mission is a job or duty we are given to accomplish. A co-mission is a task we are given to accomplish in partnership with someone else. Jesus is our partner in the *Great Commission*. He goes with us as we go to make disciples who make disciples. All authority in Heaven and earth was given to Jesus — our partner in the Great Commission!

Let's take a look at each of these commands.

1. We Are Sent – *John 20:21*

John 20:21 strongly tells that we are sent to all people groups and cultures of the world.

2. To Everyone Everywhere – *Mark 16:15*

Mark 16:15 tells that we are sent to share Christ with every man, woman and child in the world. We all have different levels of influence in our lives, made up of people we know: people we live nearby, our family and friends, and people we work with.

3. With A Strategy – *Matthew 28:18-20*

Matthew 28:18-20 gives us a strategy of how we can accomplish the Great Commission. Jesus commanded us to make disciples. *"Make disciples"* is the main focus in the Great Commission of *Matthew 28*. This means that making disciples is the major focus of the command. There are three words that tell how we are to make disciples:

- <u>Going</u> – this speaks of evangelism. Loving, sharing, serving and telling others how they can know Jesus.

- <u>Baptizing</u> – baptism is how Christ followers publicly declare their faith in Christ. They are now in relationship with others who can help them grow as a follower of Jesus. **It is important that new believers follow Christ in baptism!**

- <u>Teaching to Obey</u> – we are to teach new believers to obey all that Jesus commanded us.

4. Telling a Message – *Luke 24:44-49*

Luke 22:44-49 tells to share with others the Gospel message.

- The Gospel means "Good News." The Gospel message is the death, burial and resurrection of Christ. Below we have three case studies that share the message of the Gospel through different cultural perspectives.

  ▶ *Acts 4:12* tells that there is no other message in Heaven and on earth that men can be saved.

  ▶ *2 Corinthians 5:18-20* tells us that we are ambassadors, representing God to the world, and we are to proclaim the message of the Gospel and Jesus' love for the world.

Case Study 1: (Wilson from West Africa)

Do you know that we have sacrifices in our culture? Every tribe does. The principle behind the sacrifice is important to know. In our villages, when we encounter trouble, sickness, or famine, we enquire of the priest. The priest informs us how we have offended the spirits, and advises on an appropriate sacrifice to appease them. If we do this, the spirits will stop bothering us. Now, is it the goat, or lamb (the sacrifice) that offended the spirit? No, it is the people who have done wrong. These sacrifices are continually offered as people and societies encounter difficulties and hardships. There is no "once and for all" sacrifice. It is an endless cycle of doing what is required to temporarily appease the spirits, only to have to do it again when they are angered.

We all recognize that we have offended a Supreme God. There is One who was sent by the Supreme God: a perfect and sinless sacrifice for all of mankind. If you accept this sacrifice then the Supreme God will be appeased, once and for all. This sacrifice is Jesus. He has the power to wash away all of our sins, allowing us to stand before the Supreme God without any offence. Jesus proved through His death and resurrection, that nothing can stop Him. His power is greater than sickness and death. From the moment we place our faith in Jesus we have no need to fear, for we are saved for eternity and can have a direct relationship with Him!

Case Study 2: (Thomas from South Asia)

Our cultures are very religious and often discuss sin and punishment. For every sin and mistake there is a punishment. Our gods have come to punish sinners and save the righteous. Many think they are righteous, but if that is so, why do they continue with the religious rituals year after year? Each one of us has told at least one lie, haven't we? Year after year people go to pilgrimages, holy dips, etc. as an attempt to have our sins removed. We offer alms to the poor and charity to try to appease god. The majority of our prayers and offerings are to appease the wrath and punishment of god.

Our religious books tell us that the gods only come to save the righteous. Sinful man, regardless of his good deeds, cannot please a Holy God. So what about you and me? Who will save us?

(Case Study 2 continued)

God sent His son named Jesus, who came to earth to save the sinners. We don't have to do pilgrimages, pujas (prayers) or sacrifices for Him to save us. In fact, there is nothing we can do to earn salvation or His care and love for us. Jesus lived a completely sinless life. Even his enemies could not find one fault in Him, but still they killed him. Jesus' death as a sinless sacrifice has the ability to appease for all of our debts and sins.

His love for us caused him to sacrifice His life for us, taking our punishment for us. If we place our faith in Him, we do not need to fear because we are declared as sinless. He took the shame and punishment that we deserve and endured it in His death. He did this for you and me!

Case Study 3: (Michael from North America)

In the town that I grew up in there were many churches. Most people associated with different denominations or churches and considered themselves to be "Christian." However, many of these people had no relationship with Christ. In fact, the people inside and outside of the church often had no discernable difference at all.

Most people in our culture think that they are generally good as long as they mostly do what they are supposed to. If their good deeds outweigh their bad ones, they assume will go to heaven. The standard that they measure themselves with is usually other people who live an inferior life than they do. This makes them feel better about themselves as they try to avoid the reality of whom they truly are.

Inwardly, most people acknowledge there is something missing in their life. There is a void that they cannot fill in spite of their best efforts. There is a struggle, a pain, or a problem that is out of their control. There is a mistake, a debt, or shame that they are not able to overcome.

When people are willing to admit this I show them that in Christ there is no sin, no shame, no past mistake, no pain or hurt that is too great or that can separate us from His love. There is no height, no fear, no debt, not even death can separate us from His great love. What Jesus did on the cross was final and covers everything! His perfect life, His sacrificial death, and His glorious resurrection remind us that there is no condemnation for those who are in Christ! In response to this great love, we place Jesus at the center of our life. We respond to His limitless grace in repentance and faith that He is Greater! He is Saviour!

5. Equipped and filled for the Task – Acts 1:8

Acts 1:8 tells how believers are empowered for this mission.

- The power of the Holy Spirit is necessary. The Holy Spirit is the One who makes our witnessing successful. The results are always from God! Obedience is our responsibility.

- We must focus on witnessing in the right places. Jesus talks about Jerusalem, Judea, Samaria and the ends of the earth.

Memorize and share with five others the following statement:

We are sent... to everyone, everywhere... with a strategy... telling a message... equipped for the task by the Holy Spirit!

Planting Churches to Fulfill the Great Commission

Why is church planting so important?

1. We Plant Churches Because It Is The Most Effective Way To Fulfill The Great Commission.

- The Great Commission in *Matthew 28:18-20* is not just about evangelism, but about *making disciples* that make disciples, *baptizing* them and *teaching* them to obey all the commands of God.

- Paul's whole strategy in the New Testament was to plant churches in cities across His region. He planted churches in each village, town and city.

2. We Plant Churches to Bring Encouragement to the Body of Christ and Bring Transformation to Local Communities.

- New churches bring encouragement to all believers, as they remain faithful to Scripture.

- New churches are one of the best ways to identify and build creative, strong leaders.

- New churches are a way to meet the needs of the local community.

3. We Plant Churches Because We Are Focused on the Kingdom of God.

- Our attitude towards planting new churches is a test of whether our mindset is on our own church, or on the overall health and prosperity of the Kingdom of God in the region.

Planting new churches is the biblical way to fulfill the Great Commission.

Assignment

Read *Acts 2:41-47*. What do these verses tell you about the early church? What was important for them? Why should it be important for you as a disciple who makes disciples? What are some things you can do in response? Write your answers below:

Did you know that God wrote a Book about Church Planting?

The *Book of Acts*, the fifth book of the New Testament, is placed just after the Gospels for a reason. The Gospels teach us about Jesus. It is after we come to Christ that the power of the Holy Spirit begins to work in our lives. The entire book of *Acts* is a record of God's work in expanding the Kingdom of God through leaders who planted effective churches.

> ▶ **Who wrote *Acts*?** Luke, one of Jesus' followers.

> ▶ **Why did Luke write *Acts*?** Luke's first book, the *Gospel of Luke*, told about the life of Jesus; *Acts* is as a follow-up to that book, and talks about the birth and growth of the first Church.

> ▶ **What to look for as you read the book of *Acts*?** Evangelism, Leadership Development, The Role of the Holy Spirit, Prayer and Fasting, The Power of God at work, The Preaching of the Gospel, The Planting of Churches, Widows being Cared for, Disciples who make Disciples, and Sending out of Missionaries to the Ends of the earth.

Overview: The book of *Acts* focuses on two main leaders. The first twelve chapters of *Acts* are mostly about Peter's ministry, which was primarily with the Jewish people. The other chapters, 13-28, focus on Paul's ministry to the various cities and cultures, taking the Gospel to the Gentiles (non-Jews).

Introduction to *Acts*: The book of *Acts* could have many different titles. The official title is *The Acts of the Apostles,* because it records the early actions of Peter and all of Paul's missionary journeys. It could also be titled *The Acts of the Holy Spirit*, because the Spirit empowered all of the actions recorded in this wonderful book (*1:8*). We like to call it *The Acts of the Church Planters*, because church planting is its primary focus, especially in chapters 13-28.

Lessons from Acts 1-2

1. *1:1-8*: Jesus prepares the disciples for their task.
2. *1:12-14*: The disciples gather to pray, expecting the coming of the Holy Spirit.

3. *2:1-13*: The Spirit comes to those who had gathered to pray.

4. *2:14-41*: Peter preaches the first Gospel message.

5. *2:42-47*: The new Christian community begins to form as a church. This passage describes the earliest church:

Observation: The Apostle's Teaching

Sound doctrine and clear biblical teaching empowered by the Holy Spirit are necessary for a healthy church to grow.

> ▸ **Action Point:** On a separate page use the SWORD approach to interpret and apply *Acts 2:42-47*.

Observation: Fellowship & Breaking of Bread

A Biblical church will have people encouraging one another and helping each other. This may also refer to celebrating the Lord's Supper together.

> ▸ **Action Point:** Invite someone to share a meal with your family this week and encourage them.

Observation: Generosity and Service

The early church generously gave to people in need and served them well, both inside and outside of the church.

> ▸ **Action Point:** Identify at least one person in need from your village, perhaps a widow or orphan, and lovingly share your time and resources to assist them.

Observation: Evangelism and Outreach

The new believers kept proclaiming the Gospel, even in the midst of much persecution. They could not stop speaking about what they had seen and heard.

> ▸ **Action Point:** Go back to your list from Week 1 in your DMD book and spend time with those who have not yet accepted Christ.

Lessons from Acts 3-5

1. *3:1-10*: The Healing of the Lame Beggar near the temple.

2. *4:1-22*: Peter and John are arrested, yet they remain committed to telling others about Jesus.

3. *4:23-31*: The believers pray for boldness. They do not ask for relief from persecution, but rather for boldness to continue to speak in spite of the threats. God's Spirit filled them with power and authority and they continued to speak the Word of God with boldness.

4. *4:32-37*: The believers show great generosity.

5. *5:1-11*: Ananias and Sapphira lie to the Holy Spirit and the leadership of the church.

6. *5:17-42*: The Apostles are again put in prison.

Note: There are some people who teach that any true believer should never get sick and always be wealthy. However, Jesus and the Apostles publicly acknowledged they didn't have any money. Jesus Himself died without owning any earthly possessions, and many of the greatest church and spiritual leaders throughout history have been poor and without money or possessions. We must learn to be content with the finances God has given us (*Phil. 4:12*).

Observation: As a follower of Christ we can expect persecution. We should never give up our faith, and the only response is to trust in the Lord when we face persecution. God used persecution to form the character of Christ in His disciples. In difficult times, pray with other Christians. Don't isolate yourself.

▸ **Action Point**: When the beggar asked Peter for money, he did not have any to give. Yet, He did meet the real need of the beggar. Consider those who are in need around you. Write down one person's name and what you can do to address one of their needs.

- Name: _____

- Need to be met: _____

- How are you going to meet the need?

  _____

  _____

- Date need was met: _____

Lessons from Acts 6-8

1. *6:1-7*: Qualified leaders are chosen to serve the needs inside and outside of the church.

2. *6:8-7:60*: Stephen is arrested. He becomes the first martyr (killed for his beliefs) of the early church.

3. *8:1-3*: Saul attacks the Church. Saul began to attack the church, entering every home and taking the believers to prison. He becomes a major enemy of the church.

4. *8:4-40*: Because of persecution the church spreads to minister in new regions.

Observation: Notice the results of Stephen's death. It caused the church to begin to scatter and move into other regions. Boldly pray for your enemies. Pray for their salvation. God may have a different way of accomplishing His will than you think. Persecution could be God moving you to another area to start a church-planting center.

▶ **Action Point**: The early church had a clear plan to take care of the needy widows in their community. It was the responsibility of the church and the leadership to ensure all were being taken care of. Consider what you and your church/fellowship can do to address the needs of your community without favoritism or partiality. Give three ideas on the following page.

▶

▶

▶

Lessons from Acts 9-12

1. *9:1-19*: The conversion of Saul.

2. *9:20-31*: Saul begins to preach Christ immediately after his conversion.

3. *10:28*: God spoke to Peter in a vision that he was to go and present the Gospel of Jesus to a Gentile who lived nearby. These Gentiles had faith in Christ, and received the power and fullness of the Holy Spirit, which was a sign that God had accepted them as His people.

4. *11:19-30*: The ministry of the church at Antioch. The hand of the Lord was with these believers (v. 21) and many people came to faith in Jesus.

5. *12:1-19*: The Apostle James is killed and Peter is imprisoned and rescued.

6. *12:24*: The increase of the ministry of the Church.

Observation: God is always at work preparing our hearts to do what He wants. We should have a love for those that do not know Christ. Historically, Jews *hated* Gentiles, thinking that they were not worth saving. Perhaps you are ministering in a situation where there is hatred and distrust among various tribes or cultures. What is your response? Share the Gospel with them!

Story: There was a man named Saul (also called Paul), who was a very strict religious leader. He was unhappy with the spread of Christianity because he believed they were not worshiping the true God. So, he decided to persecute them. He approved the imprisonment and killing of believers. His goal was to destroy these people and their new faith.

One day, as he was on his way to arrest more followers of Christ, a bright light shined from Heaven and a voice asked him, "Why are you persecuting Me?" Saul replied "Who are you?" Jesus responded by again asking him "Why are you persecuting Me?" Jesus said Saul would be the instrument that He would use to reach many other peoples. After this, Saul began preaching the Gospel. This dramatic encounter with the living God caused him to tell everyone.

Read *Acts 9:1-19* and use the SWORD method of interpretation and application. Consider the questions and answers below:

1. **What do we learn about God?**

   - God loves everyone, even His enemies.

   - God is patient.

   - God has transforming power to change hearts.

2. **What do we learn about Man?**

   - The heart of man is wicked, selfish and lacks compassion.

   - Man can be sincerely wrong even when they think they are correct.

   - All sin is against God.

   - Man does not please God by simply being religious.

3. **What principles do we learn, or what sins should we avoid?**

   - When someone persecutes you, they are also persecuting Jesus. God is in perfect control.

   - God loves us for who we are, and is not impressed by our religious efforts or practice.

   - Man cannot overtake or change God's plans.

   - There may be times when God tells us to do something that we are afraid to do. God will be with us every step of the way.

4. **What commands are there to obey, or examples to follow?**

- Just as Jesus revealed Himself to Saul, He has revealed Himself to us, too. Our response: we should follow the example of Saul.

- When God tells us what to do, we must obey. Even if we are unsure or scared of the outcome.

5. **What is my response? What must I do? Application Points:**

- I will identify at least one thing God has been telling me to do that I have not obeyed. I will respond today!

  ▶ Answer: _____

  _____

- God had a clear plan and a specific goal for the life of Saul. God also has a clear plan for me. There are things He asks of me that I am sometimes unwilling to obey or follow. I must share some of these things with someone else and pray that God will help me follow fully and completely.

Lessons from Acts 13-14

1. *13:1-3*: The Antioch Church sends out Barnabas and Saul. The Spirit led the church to send them out as the first missionaries.

2. *13:4-12*: Barnabas and Saul witness everywhere they go. This is the first of Paul's three missionary journeys. It likely lasted a year and a half.

3. *13:42-52*: Paul focuses on the Gentiles. The Jews turned against him, so Paul responded by turning to the Gentiles.

4. *14:1-7*: Paul and Barnabas are rejected. Even with a fruitful ministry, there was great opposition.

5. *14:24-28*: Paul and Barnabas return to their home church. Coming home after many months of travel, Paul and Barnabas give a report to the church about all that God accomplished through their ministry.

<u>Observation</u>: *Acts 13:1-3* lists five leaders in the Church at Antioch. Notice here – and in the rest of the book of *Acts* – that the leadership of a local church involves several people, not just one leader. Having multiple leaders is the main pattern of the New Testament Church. It is fine for a church to start out with one leader. Often God calls a church planter to begin a work by himself. It is important that it not stay that way for long though. Begin to build other leaders. Give them opportunities to lead, teach and preach. Ultimately your greatest joy will be the reproduction of leaders in the life of your church. Also, if you are not actively serving in your church, begin to do so today!

<u>Observation</u>: *Acts 14:22-23* is a great summary of Church Planting. Paul and Barnabas spent their time "*strengthening the souls of the disciples, encouraging them to continue in the faith. So when they had appointed elders in every church and prayed with fasting, they commended them to the Lord in whom they had believed.*" You see the need for investing your life into others so they will become disciples who make disciples.

- Notice that it was important for Paul and Barnabas to appoint godly leaders (elders) in every church.

- Where there are several leaders, there is accountability and teamwork.

- It is important for us to report back to the people who have prayed for and financially supported us, giving reports about all that God has done.

▶ **Action Point**: In *Acts 14*, both Paul and Barnabas are called Apostles (*v. 4, 14*). This simply means '*one who is sent.*'

Are you sent by God? To whom are you sent? Write down the location and names of some people you are sent to. What will you tell them?

-

-

-

-

44

Lessons from Acts 15-18

1. *15:1-35*: A conference was held in Jerusalem to discuss conditions for Gentile membership in the church. The issue was whether Gentiles needed to become Jews in order to become Christians. Everyone concluded that they should not trouble the Gentiles with the Jewish ritual/cultural laws. James offered a proposal that Gentile Christians should avoid giving unnecessary offense.

2. *15:36-41:* Paul's second missionary journey.

3. *16:1-5:* Timothy joins Paul and Silas.

4. *16:11-17:34*: Paul and Silas witness across the region.

5. *18:1-17*: Paul goes to Corinth and finishes his missionary journey.

6. *18:18-28:* Paul and the team return to their home church.

Observation: We can learn much from the way the early Church handled the Gentile situation. There will be times in your life and ministry that you must make hard decisions. Do not act in haste. Get all the facts and prayerfully seek God's will.

Observation: Follow the leading of the Holy Spirit, even though you may not understand fully. Be creative in the ministry. Paul looked for people who were seeking God. He witnessed to people who had gathered by a river to pray (*16:11-15*). One of them, Lydia, responded to the Gospel and was baptized along with her household. You do not need a building to have a church! Be bold in your faith.

Challenge: Be known as a great student of the Bible! *Acts 17:11* says that the people in the city of Berea "*listened eagerly to Paul's message. They searched the Scriptures day after day…*"

- Witnessing for Christ is something we should all do regardless of the results. Paul only saw a few people come to faith in Athens (*17:34*), and there is no record of any miracles performed there.

Challenge: The New Testament teaches that the Christian minister is always worthy of being paid for his work in the ministry (*1 Timothy 5:18*). However, there are times when we must become creative in making money to support our involvement in the Great Commission. Paul often worked as tent maker to support his needs (*1 Corinthians 9*).

Lessons from Acts 19-22

1. *19:1-10*: Paul meets the disciples of John.

2. *19:11-22*: Paul deals with a false religion.

3. *19:23-41*: Paul experiences violent persecution.

4. *20:17-38*: Paul's message to the church elders. Paul's message here is the only example in Acts of a major speech to Christian leaders. The passage ends with great emotion as the people realized they would never see Paul again (v. 36-38).

5. *21:1-16*: Paul travels to Jerusalem. Along the way he said goodbye to many friends and received warnings from each community about the dangers facing him in Jerusalem.

6. *21:27-40*: Paul is attacked by an angry mob.

7. *22:1-21*: Paul gave his personal testimony.

Observation: Truth transforms people's lives. The spiritual battle is real. Satan is alive on earth. Satan uses some of his many evil spirits to hinder the work of God. We must stand firm against him and not fall into his temptations. *James 4:7-10* talks about resisting the enemy and remaining pure inwardly and outwardly before the Lord.

▶ **Action Point**: Memorize *James 4:7-10*. Write it below:

Challenge: Paul told the church leaders that they were to *pay careful attention* to themselves and their doctrine. In other words, ***how they lived and what they taught were two of the most critical elements in a new church***. Leaders must model the godly characteristics of the life of Jesus. They must also teach sound doctrine. You must pay close attention to live a life that is completely dedicated to Jesus and to teaching the Word of God correctly. **Memorize** *Acts 20:28*

Challenge: The devil and his demons will not be pleased that you are planting a church. They will attempt to stop your efforts, to discourage you, and perhaps even to bring persecution against you. This is where you must be strong and depend on God alone. He is your strength.

▶ **Action Point**: As we have already discussed above and in different books, one of the greatest tools in evangelism is your personal testimony of how you came to faith in Jesus. The best way to write out your testimony is to think of it in three parts:

- What your life was like before you met Jesus.

- How you came to believe in Him as your Savior. Clearly communicate the basics of the Gospel.

- How Jesus has changed you and brought you to the place you are now. Talk about the ways your life is different because of Jesus. God can use your past experiences to impact others.

Tell five more people your story this week! Write their names below:

-

-

-

-

-

47

Lessons from Acts 23-28

1. *23:1-22*: The Jews plan against Paul.

2. *25:1-27*: Paul requests to be seen by Caesar and is allowed to present his case to the King.

3. *26:1-32*: Paul testifies before King Agrippa (in fulfillment of Jesus' prophesy in *Acts 9:15*).

4. *27:1-44*: Paul travels to Rome by sea.

5. *28:1-10*: Paul witnesses on the island of Malta. Paul's time there is highlighted by his protection from a snakebite (*28:1-6*) and his healing of the local leaders' father (*28:7-10*).

6. *28:17-31*: Paul witnesses to the Jews in Rome.

Observation: God is glorified through our trials. Paul is given many opportunities to share Christ: with religious leaders (*23:1-11*), with sailors (*27:13-26*), with islanders (*28:1-10*). What opportunities is God giving you to tell others about Jesus? How have you responded? When God gives an opportunity to share the Gospel, we must be ready.

▶ **Application**: Humility should be the description of each believer. But humility does not mean that we should never stand up for our rights and the rights of others. Paul appealed for his right to a trial before the Roman emperor.

▶ **Action Point:** Consider those in your village. Is anyone being taken advantage of? Are their rights being ignored? What can you do to help stand up for their rights?

Observation: God is in control of all life. He protected Paul to fulfill His own purposes. The focus of this section of Acts is God's control, especially regarding saving Paul for his Roman testimony. Here, the Gospel continues to reach the ends of the earth (*Acts 1:8*).

Observation: Paul shared the Gospel with all who came to him, both Jews and Gentiles.

• In God's plan, Paul's time was not wasted, even when he was imprisoned. It was during his Roman imprisonment that he wrote the letters to the Ephesians, Philippians, Colossians, Philemon and Timothy.

- The very last words of the book of *Acts* tell that Paul was *"boldly proclaiming the Kingdom of God and teaching about the Lord Jesus Christ. And no one tried to stop him."* (*Acts 28:31*)

That is our prayer for you. Make disciples who make disciples and plant churches. We pray that God will open a door so wide that the Gospel will be unrestricted. We pray that your ministry will grow and expand, and that for years to come, people in your village, region and throughout your country will hear the Gospel!

Assignment

Work with your mentor and together write down a plan for you to plant a church. What are the practical steps that you need to take in order to plant a church. Consider these questions and write down your answers below.

Where are the greatest areas of need for multiple churches in your region?

How will you make sure your new church becomes a church-planting center?

How will you raise up leaders in your new church? What is your plan?'

Make it your passion and pattern to share Christ with as many as possible until Christ returns! Jesus is coming soon!

The Great Commission & Church Planting

We are empowered (*Acts 1:8*)

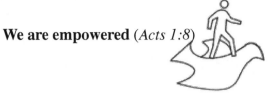

We are sent (*John 20:21*)

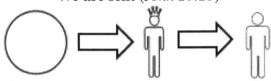

 **To everyone, everywhere** (*Mark 16:15*)

With a strategy (*Matthew 28:18-20*)

 **Telling a message — the Gospel** (*Luke 24:44-49*)

Equipped and filled for the task (*Acts 1:8*)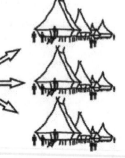

Chapter 4
Old Testament

The Old Testament is a special collection of 39 books, written between 1440 BC and about 400 BC. It tells the story of God and His people, the Jews, before the time of Jesus Christ.

These books are sometimes divided into four sections. The first section is the Law, which contains both the rules and earliest history of the Hebrew people. The second section is the record of ancient Israel's rise and decline. The third section is Poetry. This section has songs of worship, collections of wise sayings, and a story of faith. The fourth section is the Prophets. It records God's message through the men He chose to reveal His blessings, judgments, and promises.

Below are the books of the Old Testament as divided into these sections:

The Law	History	Poetry	Prophets
Genesis	Joshua	Job	Isaiah
Exodus	Judges	Psalms	Jeremiah
Leviticus	Ruth	Proverbs	Lamentations
Numbers	1 Samuel	Ecclesiastes	Ezekiel
Deuteronomy	2 Samuel	Song of Solomon	Daniel
1 Kings			Hosea
2 Kings			Joel
1 Chronicles			Amos
2 Chronicles			Obadiah
Ezra			Jonah
Nehemiah			Micah
Esther			Nahum
			Habakkuk
			Zephaniah
			Haggai
			Zechariah
			Malachi

Why should you read the Old Testament today?

1. Jesus taught the Old Testament is God's Word. It is clear that Jesus and the New Testament writers believed that the Old Testament tells God's message.

2. We should read the Old Testament to learn more about how God created His world and our faith. One of the most important verses in the whole Bible is the first. *Genesis 1:1* tells us, *"In the beginning, God created the Heavens and earth."* All that we see, and all that we have, comes from God.

3. We need to learn from the history of God's people. When God's people were faithful, God blessed them. When they were not faithful, they suffered the results of their disobedience. As you learn the lessons and stories of the Old Testament, you will see how they apply to you, even today.

4. As you read the Old Testament be sure to note God's promises, blessings and judgments. The Old Testament:

- Gives us many stories of people who learned to walk with God.
- Gives us wisdom from the very heart of God.
- Offers songs and poems that we can use to worship God today.
- Makes it clear that obeying God is not always easy, but is required for those who follow God.
- Points to the fulfilled promise we have in Jesus Christ.

Assignment

Memorize all the names of the Old Testament books.

Genesis

What do you feel or sense when you see the sky, sun, moon, mountains, ocean, and trees? Surely you sense there must be someone or something behind all of these things. Every culture has different stories about how this happened. Do you want to know what really happened? Where do we find the Truth?

The Truth is found in the Bible!

Genesis is the first book in the Bible (the first five books of the Bible called "The Law" contain the many laws God gave to His people and were written by Moses). These laws cover almost every area of life. They are the rules of how God's people understood right and wrong. These books also describe the beginning of the world and the beginning of God's people, Israel.

God is the Creator of the universe, and the Creator of His people. The title *"Genesis"* means "beginnings" or "source." The very first verse of the Bible says, *"In the beginning, God created the Heavens and earth."* The creation story follows and explains how everything we now see came into existence. (See *Genesis 1 & 2* for the whole story).

Creation finishes with God creating man and woman. We learn how sin entered the world and corrupted all of creation (*Gen. 3:1-24*). Next, we find that the sinfulness of man was so great that God decided it was good to cleanse the earth with a great flood. There was a godly man called Noah who along with his family, God chose to save from this flood. God commanded him to build an ark because a flood was coming. No one listened to Noah's warning and one day the rain came and flooded the entire earth. After a long time the rain stopped and the water went away. God promised that He would never destroy the entire earth by flood. As a sign of His promise He placed a rainbow in the sky.

After the flood, God commanded Noah and his family to be fruitful, multiply and fill the earth. As mankind grew, God told them to scatter, but they did not listen to Him. As a result, God confused their language so that each group could not understand other groups. This caused them to scatter and develop different cultures, groups, customs, and beliefs across the earth. Again wickedness grew across the world. God chose Abraham (Abram) by His grace and made a promise (covenant) between Himself and Abraham (*12:1–14:24*). Genesis' purpose is to tell the story behind God's promise (covenant) with His chosen people (Abraham's descendants).

The covenant was God's promise to make a new nation from Abraham's people; to bless all the families of the earth through him. Jesus is the Full Blessing that is found in the promise to Abraham being a blessing and having his name great. The Son of God is the Full Blessing and the Ultimate Savior of the nations. (see *Psalm 2:8*)

Genesis was written during a time when most people believed there was no single, true God above all others. Many people, especially in and around the ancient Middle East, believed in many gods with different levels of power. *Genesis* declared the power of the one true God, and that God cared about people. This book also shows that everything we see or do connects back to God, who created and sustains everything.

Exodus

Exodus continues the story of *Genesis*. Abraham's descendants traveled to Egypt during a time of famine. During that time they continued to grow and became a large nation. Gradually Egypt enslaved Israel because they feared Israel's size and strength.

Exodus tells about the rescue of Israel (Abraham's descendants are called Israel throughout the Bible) from slavery in Egypt. "*Exodus*" means "going out" or "exit." The purpose of *Exodus* is to connect and continue God's promise with Abraham (*Gen. 12:2*) through a new promise with Moses (*Ex. 19:5*). God used Moses as the deliverer and leader of his people out of slavery. The people of Egypt worshiped many false gods. As a result, God showed himself as the All-Powerful Most High God by defeating the powers and gods that were feared and worshiped in Egypt. God did this by empowering Moses to defeat the leaders of Egypt.

▸ Action Point: Read *Exodus 7:14-14:31*. Write down at least eleven ways that God defeated the Egyptians and their gods.

    1.

    2.

    3.

    4.

    5.

6.

7.

8.

9.

10.

11.

The Ten Plagues on Egypt

The Plague	Location
Blood	*Exodus 7:22*
Frogs	*Exodus 8:6*
Lice	*Exodus 8:17*
Flies	*Exodus 8:24*
Diseased livestock	*Exodus 9:6*
Boils	*Exodus 9:10*
Hail	*Exodus 9:23*
Locusts	*Exodus 10:13*
Darkness	*Exodus 10:22*
Death of firstborn	*Exodus 12:29*

Exodus also records Israel's beginnings as a nation, operating under God's laws and covenant during its wilderness journey towards the land that God promised to Abraham and his descendants. The theme for Exodus is Israel's change from a captive (slaves) people in Egypt into a covenant nation under the leadership of God. God spoke to Moses and told him to remind the people of Israel how He had saved them from slavery. He called on the people to obey God and be faithful to Him, worship Him and He would be their God. God also provided laws and commands on how to live and what to do in order to remain in a healthy and right relationship.

Leviticus

In *Leviticus*, God shows His desire to have fellowship with Israel. Leviticus provides and explains the laws God's people needed to follow to live in fellowship with God. The last chapters of *Exodus* tell about the building of the tabernacle (this was Israel's house of worship: see *Ex. 25-40*). *Leviticus* begins with descriptions of the sacrifices to be performed in the tabernacle (*Lev. 1-7*). *Leviticus* explains how important these sacrifices are to keep relationship with God. (Before Jesus, sacrifices were required by God's Holiness and Law to take the punishment of their sins away temporarily. Remember that Jesus was the final sacrifice and is the way we have a relationship with God.)

"*Leviticus*" means "having to do with the priests" (Levites). The purpose of *Leviticus* was to show the people of Israel (Israelites) how they could both worship and live for God in purity. The theme of *Leviticus* is holiness (see *19:2*). Holiness in worship (*chapters 1-17*), and holiness in everyday life (*chapters 18-27*).

Observation: Consider your culture and customs. How do your people view sacrifices? How have you experienced this in the past? What were some thoughts that came to mind when you observed or even participated in these rituals? Look at *Hebrews 10:10, 14*. God's will was for us to be made holy by the sacrifice of Jesus Christ on the cross—**once for all time**. This offering, Jesus, forever paid the price for those who trust in Him.

Numbers

Numbers tells about Israel's wandering in the wilderness. It describes a major transition in the history of God's people. *Numbers* records the death of the first generation of freed slaves from Egypt (*chapters 1-25*), and the life of the second wilderness generation (*chapters 26-36*). "*Numbers*" gets its name from all the counting and numbers in the book.

The purpose of *Numbers* was to describe the change from Israel's old generation that left Egypt and disobeyed God in the desert to the new generation that is near the land that God promised Abraham (Promised Land). The main theme of *Numbers* is that God's people can go forward only as far as they trust God. For example:

> Moses led the people of Israel through the wilderness for many years. When they finally reached the border of the land God had promised them, Moses sent in twelve men to view and observe the land. They found it was fertile and beautiful, but the people who lived there were powerful. Of the twelve men sent, only two thought they would be able to overtake the local people with God's strength. When they returned to their camp they reported to Moses what they had seen. There was a debate among God's people, doubting that they were able to take the land. This resulted in the people rebelling against God's direction and commands. Due to their lack of faith in God, this entire generation was not able to enter this beautiful land except these two men, Joshua & Caleb, who believed in God. (For the full story see *Numbers 13-14*).

Numbers begins just 13 months after Israel left Egypt and ends almost 39 years later. Numbers shows that God is angry with anyone who approaches Him with rebellion or immorality (*13:1-14:45*). Numbers also reveals how God provided for His people's needs (God gave them food and water in the desert for 40 years). The book of *Numbers* says that God is holy, and shows that it is very important to approach God in the right way.

▶ **Question**: Read *John 14:6*. What is the proper way to approach God today? Write your answer

▶ **Action Point**: What is one way you can actively and fully trust God today? Is there something God has been telling you to do that you have doubted? Write it below and pray for boldness:

Deuteronomy

Deuteronomy records the last messages from Moses to the generation of Israelites about to enter the Promised Land. Moses encouraged this new generation not to disobey God like the generation before them had done. He urged them to remember it was not by their good works or might that they received this promise, but only by God's love and grace (*7:6-11*).

Deuteronomy tells of the renewed promise (covenant) between God and His people, and focuses on love for God, not rules and rituals to God. *Deuteronomy* ends with the transition of leadership from Moses to Joshua (*chapters 31-34*).

The name "*Deuteronomy*" means "second law." It explains God's Law to a second generation of Israelites. The purpose of *Deuteronomy* was to encourage God's people to make a fresh commitment to the Lord.

> ▸ **Question**: Consider your commitment to the Lord. What are the areas of your life that you have not given to God completely? Are you willing to give yourself completely to God?

Joshua

Joshua is the first of the twelve historical books in the Old Testament. These twelve books cover about 700 years of history beginning with Israel entering the Promised Land and ending with the return of the Jewish nation from Babylon. The purpose was to show how God fulfilled His promise to give Israel the land of Canaan (the Promised Land, *1:2-6; 21:43*). Joshua's name means: "The Lord Saves." Joshua was Moses' disciple. There are many times in *Joshua* where God works miracles to help Israel defeat its enemies. The following story tells one such account:

> After Moses' death, Joshua became the leader of the Israelites. As they took the land God promised, there was a large city named Jericho with big walls that were impossible to overtake. Joshua sent two spies to get an understanding of the city. They hid from the local authorities in the home of a prostitute by the name of Rahab. Everyone knew that God was going to give the Israelites the city and Jericho would be destroyed. Rahab asked, "Can you spare me and my family?" They told her that when the

time came for the Israelites to attack, to hang out a red ribbon from her window and she and her family would be spared. God told Joshua to trust him by walking around the city one time each day for seven days. On the seventh day God instructed the Israelites to walk around the city seven times and when they did this, the walls fell down and they overtook the city. Of the entire city only Rahab and her family were spared. (Read *chapters 2 and 6* for the full story.)

▶ **Question**: Why were the people of Jericho scared of the Israelites? Out of all of Jericho, only Rahab and her family were spared. Why do you think this happened? What do you learn from this?

Observation: The plan that God gave to Joshua may have seemed like a strange and foolish idea. Obedience to God's plan brought about victory for Joshua and his people. We should never doubt God, and remember Him when victory comes.

▶ **Action Point**: Tell this story and the lessons you learned to two people this week.

Judges

Judges is another historical book. It tells about God rescuing the nation of Israel through several bold leaders called "judges." These judges did not always have an official title or role of leadership, but were simply used by God for fulfilling His purposes. They often combined the roles of military leader and governor. They were the leaders God used after Joshua's death and before God appointed kings to rule His people. In total there were 15 judges across 300+ years. During the time of *Judges*, the people of Israel constantly disobeyed God and did what was good in their own eyes. As a result they almost destroyed themselves on many occasions.

The book of *Judges* is named for the judges God appointed to lead His people and emphasizes the importance of God's mercy and grace. The purpose of *Judges* was to show the results of disobedience to God, and finally the need for a righteous king who would lead Israel to God. The themes are the ongoing disobedience of Israel as they fail to learn from their mistakes. The message in *Judges* is developed through seven cycles of oppression and deliverance (*chapters 3-16*). Each cycle had five parts or steps:

1. Israel's sin.
2. Israel is oppressed.
3. Israel cries out to God for help.
4. God uses a judge to save the people of Israel.
5. Israel enters into a time of rest.

For example consider this story:

> The people of Israel continued to disobey God. As a result they experienced 40 years of oppression by a group of people called the Philistines. After this time God brought about a judge named Samson. As the young man grew, the Lord blessed him and the Spirit of the Lord began to work in his life. God used Samson to remove the power of the Philistines from His people (*Judges 13-16*).

Assignment

Read about another judge named Gideon and write down the five cycles of oppression and deliverance (See *Judges 6-8*.) Also note how God was able to use Gideon to conquer his enemies in spite of his fear.

1.

2.

3.

4.

5.

Ruth

The book of *Ruth* is a story of a young girl named Ruth who married into a different culture. Her husband was an Israelite whose family moved out of Israel during a time of famine. While they were there, life was difficult. Ruth lost her husband, father-in-law, and brother-in-law, but decided to stay and care for her mother-in-law, Naomi. After some time Naomi decided to return home to Israel. Ruth did not want to leave her mother-in-law alone, so urged by love and compassion Ruth decided to join her. She said *"your home will be my home, and your God will be my God, where you die, I will die."* (*Ruth 1:16, 17*)

> When they returned to Israel it was harvest time. Ruth collected grain from a nearby land owned by Boaz, a relative of Naomi's husband. Boaz helped Ruth regain the land that was rightfully her husband's property. Boaz became Ruth's husband and together they had a son. The women of the town said to Naomi, *"Praise the Lord, who has now provided a redeemer for your family! May this child be famous in Israel. May he restore your youth and care for you in your old age. For he is the son of your daughter-in-law who loves you and has been better to you than seven sons!"*(*Ruth 4:14, 15*) From this lineage (family line) came King David and later Jesus (See *Ruth 1-4* for the full story).

<u>Observation</u>: Ruth was a woman who left her home and her heritage in exchange for a life with the people and God of Israel. The purpose of *Ruth* is to show God's loving care. He is always watching and working, even though we don't always see Him. The themes in *Ruth* are redemption and God's desire for all people to believe in Him.

1 Samuel

1 Samuel covers the ninety-four year period from Samuel's birth (Israel's last Judge) to Saul's death (Israel's first King). Samuel lived around the same period as Ruth. *The books of Samuel* are named for the prophet Samuel, who is a main character. The books also include the change in Israel from the time of Judges to the time of Kings.

God used Samuel as the last judge to transition Israel from Judges to Kings. The people of Israel grew tired of judges and compared themselves to other nations who were ruled by powerful kings. Even though God was their true King, Israel failed to recognize His leadership and wanted a human king to represent them. God gave Samuel the responsibility to appoint a King. According to God's direction Samuel appointed Saul and David, the first and second Kings of Israel.

The themes of *1 Samuel* show how the consequences of sin affect rulers as much as anyone else (see *15:23*). *1 Samuel* tells the story of the lives of the prophet Samuel (*chapters 1-7*), Israel's first king, Saul (*chapters 8-31*), and David, Israel's greatest king who was yet to be crowned (*chapters 16-31*).

2 Samuel

2 Samuel tells about David's rule as King. It records the major events of David's fourty year reign. *2 Samuel* also records David's sins of adultery, murder and the effects of those sins on David's family and his overall leadership.

The purpose of *2 Samuel* continues from *1 Samuel*: to show how God's authority over Israel was shown specifically, through the rise and rule of King David.

Observation: **This book makes it clear that God was still the true King of Israel**. The theme of *2 Samuel* is that the key to David's reign, when it was successful, was David's relationship with God. Samuel makes it clear that obedience to God brings blessing, while disobedience brings trouble. **This is not to say that obedience always brings about the results we want**. Obedience brings the blessing of a closer relationship with God. Disobedience puts distance in our relationship with God. Being faithful to God can take us through the most difficult situations.

- God's promise to David and his descendants is one example of God's grace and mercy staying with a person even though sin may bring trouble (7:14-15).

- David's example demonstrates the power of repentance in restoring our relationship with God (12:13-14, 24-31).

- David's example also demonstrates that there are always consequences to sin (12:15-23).

▶ **Question**: Who is the King of your life? Even when you sin or disobey God, what should your response be? Remember, **obedience brings the blessing of a closer relationship with God!**

1 & 2 Kings

1 and 2 Kings were originally one book. Together, they offer a political history of Israel from the time of Solomon (King David's son), until the beginning of the Babylonian captivity. *Kings* tells about the rule of Solomon over the people of Israel. After Solomon's death in *1 Kings, chapter 11*, the people of Israel were divided into two kingdoms: Judah (in the South) and Israel (in the North).

Remember the first promise God gave to Abraham: *that from his off-spring God would bless the world*. From Abraham came Isaac and from Isaac came Jacob. Jacob had four wives. Between them, they bore Jacob twelve sons who would father the twelve tribes of Israel. Jacob was also called Israel.

The tribes that are included in Judah (South Kingdom) are: Judah and Benjamin.

The tribes that are included in Israel (North Kingdom) are: Reuben, Simeon, Issachar, Zebulun, Dan, Naphtali, Gad, Asher, Ephraim, and Manasseh.

The message of *1 and 2 Kings* is to record both the history of the kings of Israel (North Kingdom had 19 kings) and Judah (South Kingdom had 20 kings), along with the spiritual lessons learned from their rule.

Observations:

- A divided heart and disobedience resulted in a divided kingdom and God's judgment.
- There is a difference between God's standards and the world's standards.
- Kings are just as responsible to live by God's standards as anyone else.
- God is always ready to help those who turn to Him. He is faithful even when we are not.

2 Kings ends with the destruction of the Northern Kingdom by the Assyrians, and the Southern Kingdom's captivity by the Babylonians. It is important to recognize that the Babylonians destroyed God's Temple that was built by Solomon. After some time, Babylon was taken over by the Persians. The captives from Judah (Southern Kingdom) were allowed to return home after 70 years.

1 & 2 Chronicles

The *Chronicles* cover the same time of history as *2 Samuel* to *2 Kings*. *Chronicles* tells about this history from the perspective of the Jews (Southern Kingdom) who returned from exile in Persia to rebuild Jerusalem.

God established David's kingdom because of His promises to Abraham, Isaac and Jacob (*17:12*). The purpose of *1 Chronicles* was to inspire those who remained from Judah (who had returned to Jerusalem to rebuild their nation and God's Temple).

1 Chronicles first tells about David's family line all the way back to the first man, Adam. Then it tells about David's rule as king of Israel. *1 Chronicles* shows that God alone deserves our worship, prayer, and honor (see *16:29; 17:20*). It also shows that true worship of God connects us with generations of God's people of faith (*17:21-22*; see *Heb. 11*). God's faithfulness to His promises were true for David and are true for all generations of His people (*16:14-24*), including you!

2 Chronicles continues the story and tells about the dedication, weakening, and ruin of the temple. *2 Chronicles* has two major sections: the first section (*chapters 1-9*), tells about Solomon's rule as king. The second section (*chapters 10-36*), tells about the many kings of the divided kingdoms of Israel and Judah.

Observation: Chronicles tells us about God's faithfulness in keeping His promises to David. It tells about the temple, Levites, priests, and ways to worship (*20:18-22*).

Observation: Prayer and worship are important parts in the life of every believer. To God, worship and right relationship with Him are more important than anything else. Obedience to God is a true form of worship.

> ▶ **Action Point**: Are you worshiping Jesus and Jesus alone? How is your prayer life? Write a prayer to God below.

Ezra

The book of *Ezra* tells about God fulfilling His promises to bring His people back and rebuild Jerusalem and God's temple.

This book is named for Ezra, a priest who was an expert on the Law of Moses (*7:6*). Ezra led a group of Jewish exiles from Babylon to Jerusalem to help rebuild the temple, the city, and the Jewish community. The purpose of *Ezra* is to encourage the Jews who had returned to practice true worship and true obedience to God. It also shows God's faithfulness and how He restored the people to their land.

Observation: Ezra had a strong desire to know, understand and teach the Word of God accurately. We too should follow his example.

Nehemiah

The book of *Nehemiah* tells about the rebuilding of Jerusalem's walls after the Jewish exiles returned from Babylon. The book is named after Nehemiah, who led the return of Jewish exiles to their homeland. Nehemiah led the project of rebuilding the exterior walls of Jerusalem, and rebuilding the community of God's people.

> Nehemiah was among the exiled Jews and worked in the palace of the king of Persia. When he heard news from Jerusalem concerning the suffering and destruction of his homeland, he prayed and asked God to act on his behalf. God heard his prayer and touched the heart of the king. The king gave Nehemiah permission and resources to go back and rebuild the walls of Jerusalem and meet the needs of his people.

> When Nehemiah went to Jerusalem he faced many obstacles. He responded by praying for his enemies, and taught his people to focus on unity so they could succeed in their task. He was successful in rebuilding the walls in only 52 days! The surrounding nations, who had mocked their efforts to rebuild the walls, rec-

ognized that what they accomplished was done by the hand of God. Nehemiah confirmed this, telling others that the "*gracious hand of God*" was on him. (*Nehemiah 2:18*)

Observation: When we see the physical and spiritual needs of the people around us, it should motivate us towards prayer, care and sharing the love of Christ.

▶   **Action Point**: Are there any people in your area that are suffering or struggling? What is one thing you can do for them this week? Write your answer:

Observation: The book of Nehemiah demonstrates how important a godly leader can be. Great men and women of God will see fruit when they trust God. A godly leader sees God do the impossible.

Esther

The book of *Esther* is a wonderful story of God's care for His people while they were under Persian rule. It tells of the bravery of Esther who stood up for her people at a time when they faced destruction.

> There was a king who was looking for a wife across his kingdom. There was a beautiful Jewish girl named Esther. The king took Esther as his wife and she became his queen. A time came that she received word from her uncle that her native people, the Jews, were facing trouble. She risked her life to influence the king to assist her people.

The purpose of Esther was to remind the returned Jewish exiles that God was faithful to keep His promises to Israel. The key theme in Esther is God's promised loyalty to Israel, even in a land that did not fear God or care about the Jews.

<u>Observation</u>: Esther's love for her people and her faith in God brought deliverance for her people.

> ▶ **Question**: Are you willing to act on behalf of your friends, family, and neighbors?

> ▶ **Action Point**: What is one way you can show love for these people?

Job

There was a man named Job, who was very powerful, wealthy and loved God. He had many friends, children and possessions. He worshiped God with all his heart and without compromise.

One day Satan approached God and said that Job only worshiped God because of the material and physical blessings God had given him. As a result, God allowed Satan to remove everything from Job, including: his wealth, land, animals, family, and even his health.

Job faced incredible discouragement. During this time his friends told him that if he were a righteous man none of these things would have happened. Job responded that it is God who gives and God who takes away. Through all these trials, Job remained faithful and trusted God. He learned that God is in control and does not need explain why He does what he does. In response to Job's faithfulness God restored Job.

The book of *Job* is the one of five Poetry & Wisdom books in the Old Testament. The others are *Psalms, Proverbs, Ecclesiastes,* and *Song of Solomon*. The book of Job deals with a question almost everyone asks: "Why does God allow suffering?" The book shows that this question is too big for us. The only response possible is that God is in control and works in ways that man does not always understand or agree with. However, we do know that God works all things for the good of those who love Him and are called according to His purposes (*Rom. 8:28*).

<u>Observation</u>: Job learned through his suffering. God is the Supreme Ruler over the entire universe, including our lives, regardless of our situation. Job's story can help us understand God's view on suffering. Job is the oldest book in the Bible.

Psalms

The book of *Psalms* is often called the heart of the Old Testament. It is full of God pouring His heart out to man, and man pouring his heart out to God. It is a collection of individual poems that were written to be sung with instrumental music. The poems tell about many different kinds of life experiences. Each of them offers some kind of praise or prayer to God. Parts of the book of *Psalms* were used as a songbook in ancient Israel for their worship services.

The *Psalms* have a number of different writers. In most of the 150 psalms, the author's name is listed before the psalm he wrote. King David is the author of 75 psalms. Moses wrote at least one psalm. Solomon wrote two psalms. Some of the men David put in charge of worship in Israel while he was king wrote psalms in this book.

The dates of the individual psalms range nearly 1,000 years apart. **The purpose of *Psalms* is to lead people into the worship, praise, and confession of the one true God.**

A brief description of the different *Psalms*:

1. *Psalms 1-41* contains the overall topics of man and creation.

2. *Psalms 42-72* tells about the overall topics of rescue and redemption.

3. *Psalms 73-89* covers the topics of worship and holiness.

4. *Psalms 90-106* tells about wilderness and wandering.

5. *Psalms 107-150* contains the overall topics of the Word of God and worship.

Observation: **The book of Psalms shows how to connect almost every situation in life with a reason to worship God**. Many Psalms are examples of praising God at all times and all situations (*34:1*). It is important to find reasons to thank God in all situations.

▶ **Action Point**: Reflect on a difficult situation that you are facing and consider how you may praise God in response!

Read and memorize *Psalm 23* written below:

The Lord is my shepherd; I have all that I need. He lets me rest in green meadows; He leads me beside peaceful streams. He renews my strength. He guides me along right paths, bringing honor to His name. Even when I walk through the darkest valley, I will not be afraid, for You are close beside me. Your rod and Your staff protect and comfort me. You prepare a feast for me in the presence of my enemies. You honor me by anointing my head with oil. My cup overflows with blessings. Surely Your goodness and unfailing love will pursue me all the days of my life, and I will live in the house of the Lord forever.

Proverbs

Before you begin, write down two or three proverbs taught in your culture in relation to God.

1.

2.

3.

The book of *Proverbs* tells how faith in God and obedience to His Word is applied in day-to-day life. *Proverbs* makes right and wrong conduct clear for many situations. *Proverbs* is an example of wisdom literature in the Old Testament. Wisdom literature describes thoughts about life in memorable forms.

Observation: The purpose of *Proverbs* is to tell about the importance of a pure heart and a clear mind in order to honor and obey God in everyday life (*1:2-6*). The main theme of Proverbs is Godly wisdom (proper living according to God's Word and ways) begins with the fear of the Lord (*9:10*).

> ▶ **Action Point**: Memorize the following verses:
>   - *Proverbs 1:10*
>   - *Proverbs 3:5-6*
>   - *Proverbs 21:31*

Ecclesiastes

King Solomon had everything one person could ever want or need. He was richer and wiser than any other person in the past or present (He had more than 22,679 kilograms of gold). Even though he had all of these possessions, he considered it all vanity and worthless without God.

The book of *Ecclesiastes* tells about the search for meaning in life. It says that every area in life – work, wealth, wisdom, righteousness, and youth – are empty and temporary. It shows the limitations of human work and wisdom. *Ecclesiastes* also shows that when humans see their limitations, they can be free to live in respect and awe of God. The word *Ecclesiastes* means "one who calls an assembly."

The purpose of *Ecclesiastes* is to show the emptiness of every part of life without God. Some believe that king Solomon may have written Ecclesiastes to teach other nations about their need for God.

The theme of *Ecclesiastes* is that the search for life's meaning in human activity is worthless. **Life has meaning only when we see it with God as the main focus**. The fear of the Lord is necessary to godly living in this book and in our life today.

Song of Solomon

Song of Solomon (also known as *Song of Songs*) is a collection of love poems and songs. The book shows that love, including sexual love within marriage, is a gift from God. It also shows how love within a faithful marriage grows and matures.

The title of the book comes from its literary form (songs), and from its author Solomon. The purpose of *Song of Solomon* is to commend sexual love between a man and woman in marriage. The theme of *Song of Solomon* is human love that can be blessed and celebrated in a godly relationship. This love has its freedoms in marriage as the couple chooses, however, it is only inside the marriage relationship and it is only between the same man and same woman, bonded before the Lord in marriage.

Isaiah

The book of *Isaiah* is the first of sixteen books of the prophets in the Old Testament. A prophet in the Old Testament was someone who spoke on behalf of God and was a channel that God used to speak to mankind.

> Isaiah was the friend of a king. He had access to a great palace and enjoyed a nice life. One day the king died and Isaiah had a vision about God, the King of the Universe sitting on the throne. In this vision he realized that God was the true King and cried out to God that he was a sinful man. God cleansed him and Isaiah heard a voice asking, "Who will go for me?" He responded, "Here am I, send me." Thereafter he began to speak on behalf of God. (See *Isaiah 6* for the whole story)
>
> Many times God told Isaiah to warn the people to turn from their sins or they would face judgment. Isaiah was given the task to communicate this difficult truth to those who often times refused to listen. God would also illustrate the coming judgment by having Isaiah do some strange and difficult actions. Isaiah obeyed because he knew it was from God. This was the attitude a prophet of God should have.

Observation: We too should have an attitude that trusts God completely, obeying immediately and fully.

Isaiah tells about Isaiah's life and his prophecies. God called Isaiah to a long and prophetic ministry. Isaiah spoke from Jerusalem to several groups and nations over a 60-year period. The book of *Isaiah* also contains more prophecies about Jesus than any other Old Testament book except the *Psalms*.

Isaiah's name means Salvation is of the Lord. The purposes of *Isaiah* were to remind God's people of their special relationship with God as a part of His covenant, and to call the nation of Judah back to God.

The general theme of *Isaiah* is that salvation comes from the Lord; and those who follow obediently after God will experience that salvation one day. Of all the prophetic books in the Old Testament, *Isaiah* has the largest number of prophecies about Jesus. The book of *Isaiah* tells about:

- Christ's birth to a virgin (*Isa. 7:14; Luke. 1:26-31*).
- His miracles (*Isa. 35:5-6; Mt. 12:22; Luke. 4:18; 7:22*).
- His obedience (*Isa. 50:5; Mt. 26:39*).
- His message (*Isa. 61:1-2; Luke. 4:18-19*).
- His suffering and death (*Isa. 50:6; 53:1-12; Mt. 27:26, 30*).
- His exaltation (*Isa. 52:13; Rom. 4:24-25; Phi. 2:9-11*).

Jeremiah

The book of *Jeremiah* is filled with warnings to people whose hearts were no longer focused on God. *Jeremiah* tells about the last fifty years of Judah before they were conquered by Babylon. It is mostly a sad story, and the sadness of the priest and prophet Jeremiah for his people is clear. Even though the people of Judah had access to worship in the temple and had the one true religion, they still needed to obey their promises with God or face disaster.

The title of this book comes from the name of the prophet Jeremiah, which means "The Lord establishes." The purpose of the book of *Jeremiah* was to remind Judah that disobedience to God's promises would bring them disaster. Only a commitment to obeying God would save them from His judgment.

The theme of *Jeremiah* is God's judgment, first on Judah and then on the nations of the world. Jeremiah basically had one person, named Baruch, to mentor who was faithful to God. The people of his hometown and even his own family persecuted him. Ultimately the entire area ignored or persecuted him, but he still stood firm.

> ▸ **Question**: How would you respond if only one person fol-
> lowed the Lord in your ministry? What about if your own town
> and family reject, persecute, and imprison you because of your
> faith in Christ?

Lamentations

Jeremiah also wrote the book of *Lamentations*, which shows his intense
grief when Jerusalem fell to Babylon. *Lamentations* is about the suffering of a nation (Judah). The title for *Lamentations* is taken from the first
word in the book, which is a "lament" or expression of mourning and
sadness. Both before and after God's punishment on Judah, Jeremiah
wept for his people because of love and compassion.

It would have been easy for Jeremiah and the Jews to lose all hope. But
in *Lamentations 3:21-31*, Jeremiah remembers that God will not forget
His people forever:

> *Yet I still dare to hope when I remember this: The faithful love of
> the Lord never ends! His mercies never cease. Great is His faith-
> fulness; His mercies begin afresh each morning. I say to myself,
> "The Lord is my inheritance; therefore, I will hope in Him!" The
> Lord is good to those who depend on Him, to those who search
> for him. So it is good to wait quietly for salvation from the Lord.
> And it is good for people to submit at an early age to the yoke of
> His discipline. Let them sit alone in silence beneath the Lord's
> demands. Let them lie face down in the dust, for there may be
> hope at last. Let them turn the other cheek to those who strike
> them and accept the insults of their enemies. For no one is aban-
> doned by the Lord forever.*

The purpose of *Lamentations* was to show some of the reasons for, and
results of, suffering. It also shows how God uses suffering for His purposes. The general theme in *Lamentations* is the faithfulness of God in
difficult times.

> ▸ **Question**: How has God been faithful when you have experi-
> enced difficult times? Write some examples.

Ezekiel

The book of *Ezekiel* tells about the ministry of Ezekiel the prophet. Ezekiel was in the first group of Jewish exiles in Babylon. He preached to the exiled Jews at the same time Jeremiah was warning the remaining Jews in Jerusalem about the coming judgment against them. Ezekiel's name means "God strengthens."

The purpose of *Ezekiel* was to remind the exiles in Babylon that God had not forgotten them, even though they were far away from the temple and the Promised Land. God cares for His people no matter where they are. The theme of *Ezekiel* is that the purpose of God's grace and discipline always results in spiritual maturity.

▶ **Question**: How do you respond to God's discipline?

Daniel

The book of *Daniel* tells the story of Daniel, a Jewish exile who became a court official in Babylon. Daniel served as a close advisor to both the Babylonian king Nebuchadnezzar and to Cyrus, the Persian king who conquered Babylon.

> Daniel and his three friends were put in a position of leadership in the Babylonian kingdom. This brought about jealousy from some of the king's advisors. So, they recommended that the king make a statue of himself and sign a decree that all the people worship the statue. Those that disobeyed would be thrown into a pit of fire. They purposely did this because they knew these three friends of Daniel would not bow to the statue. By worshiping the statue they were indirectly worshiping the king instead of the One True God. These three friends decided not to bow to this statue and disobey the order of the king. When the trumpet sounded to worship the statue, they did not bow. The king's advisors told of their actions. They were brought before the king and questioned as to why they refused to bow to the statue. They told the king respectfully that they could not bow before anyone but the One True God. The king was angry and ordered that they be put into the fire. The three friends boldly stated "Our God can save us from this fire, but even if He doesn't we will never worship this statue."

The king ordered the fire so hot that the guards who threw the three friends in the fire were burned alive. After the three friends were thrown the fire, the king was astonished because he saw four instead of three people and they were walking freely! The king ordered them released from the fire. When they came out, there was not even a hint of smoke on their clothes. (See *chapter 3* for the whole story)

Later we find Daniel facing more trials. One story tells how king Darius declared that all people should worship him alone. Daniel, being a child of God, decided to follow after God. It was reported that he continued to pray to God, rather than bow to the king. The punishment for refusing to worship the king was being thrown into a pit of lions. Daniel was put into the pit, but God protected Daniel by shutting the mouths of the lions and protecting him the entire night. The hungry lions did not touch him. This proved to the king and all the people that the God Daniel served was the true God. Even the king made a decree that all people should worship and fear the God of Daniel. (See *chapter 6* for the whole story)

The book of *Daniel* is named for Daniel, whose name means "God is my Judge." The purpose of *Daniel* is to show how God works out His purposes even in a foreign land.

The themes in *Daniel* are God's faithfulness to His promises even when His people were in exile; and God's authority over all nations.

▶ **Question**: How faithful are you when you face persecution and pressures from different people? Are you serious about following God?

Hosea

When the prophet Hosea began his ministry, God told him to marry an unfaithful woman. Their marriage was to show how Israel was unfaithful to God.

▶ **Question**: Consider the shame that Hosea must have felt in obeying God in this situation. What would you have done?

The book of *Hosea* tells about Hosea's ministry in the northern kingdom of Israel in the years before its fall to Assyria. It also tells about God's hatred of sin. Yet, as Hosea restores his wife Gomer, God gives him the message that Israel, too, would be restored.

Hosea's name means "salvation." The purpose of *Hosea* was to condemn sin, warn Israel of God's coming judgment, and to remind the loyal people of God that His love would restore them. The theme of *Hosea* is that Israel's special relationship with God is like a marriage. Like a marriage, both partners need to honor the commitment. The first part of *Hosea* is the story of an unfaithful wife, Gomer, and her faithful husband Hosea (*1-3*). The second part is the story of an unfaithful Israel and their faithful God (*4-14*).

Joel

Joel is a short book with a clear message of warning for God's people. *Joel* uses a recent plague as an example to describe what the coming judgment of God against Judah will be like. *Joel* also tells God's people to repent, and offers hope in the day of salvation that follows judgment. The name Joel means "Yahweh is God."

The purposes of the book of *Joel* is to call the nation of Judah to repentance (*2:1-3:17*), and to comfort the faithful with the promises of salvation (*3:18-21*). The theme of *Joel* is the coming **Day of the Lord**, which is a time when God will destroy His enemies and save Israel.

Amos

The book of *Amos* tells about the ministry of Amos, a shepherd, who prophesied against the injustice and self-centered wealth in the northern kingdom of Israel. Amos spoke that God's judgment was coming because the poor in Israel were ignored and mistreated (even sold into slavery). Amos means "Burden-bearer."

The purpose of the book of *Amos* was to call the leaders in Israel to repent and change their behavior toward the poor:

> *This is what the Lord says: "The people of Israel have sinned again and again, and I will not let them go unpunished! They*

sell honorable people for silver and poor people for a pair of sandals. They trample helpless people in the dust and shove the oppressed out of the way. Both father and son sleep with the same woman, corrupting my holy name. At their religious festivals, they lounge in clothing their debtors put up as security. In the house of their gods, they drink wine bought with unjust fines. (Amos 2:6-8)

The main theme in *Amos* is God's call to justice. God was angry that people forgot their need to treat others according to their covenant with Him. If God was righteous and just, His people needed to be righteous and just. See *Amos 5:18-27*:

What sorrow awaits you who say, "If only the day of the Lord were here!" You have no idea what you are wishing for. That day will bring darkness, not light. In that day you will be like a man who runs from a lion — only to meet a bear. Escaping from the bear, he leans his hand against a wall in his house — and he's bitten by a snake. Yes, the day of the Lord will be dark and hopeless, without a ray of joy or hope. "I hate all your show and pretense — the hypocrisy of your religious festivals and solemn assemblies. I will not accept your burnt offerings and grain offerings. I won't even notice all your choice peace offerings. Away with your noisy hymns of praise! I will not listen to the music of your harps. Instead, I want to see a mighty flood of justice, an endless river of righteous living. "Was it to me you were bringing sacrifices and offerings during the forty years in the wilderness, Israel? No, you served your pagan gods—Sakkuth your king god and Kaiwan your star god—the images you made for yourselves. So I will send you into exile..." says the Lord, whose name is the God of Heaven's Armies.

▸ **Question**: How do you treat those around you in need? God requires His character to be reflected in His people. Are you reflecting His character in your everyday life? When people see your character and actions can they see Christ?

Obadiah

The book of *Obadiah* is the shortest Old Testament book, and tells about the struggle between Edom and the people of Israel. The Edomites were from the family line of Esau, Jacob's brother. Edom and Israel were usually in some kind of fight with each other. *Obadiah* says that Edom would be completely destroyed because it always chose to stand against God's chosen people.

Obadiah means "Servant of the Lord." The purpose of *Obadiah* is to say that God rules over all nations, whether they honor Him or not. This truth provided comfort to the faithful as it reminded them that God had not abandoned them. *Obadiah* expresses a very strong statement of judgment, and that is the theme of the book. God will completely destroy Edom, and restore Judah.

Obadiah ends with a promise for future blessings for Israel:

> *"Then my people...will occupy the mountains of Edom. Those living in the foothills of Judah will possess the Philistine plains and take over the fields of Ephraim and Samaria. And the people of Benjamin will occupy the land of Gilead. The exiles of Israel will return to their land...The captives from Jerusalem exiled in the north will return home...Those who have been rescued will go up to Mount Zion in Jerusalem to rule over the mountains of Edom. And the LORD himself will be king!" (verses 19-21).*

Jonah

The book of *Jonah* tells about the prophet Jonah (who served for 35 years as a prophet in the Northern Kingdom) and his mission to Nineveh, a wicked and cruel city with a wicked king. Jonah shows that God's mercy goes beyond His chosen people into the entire world. It also shows that God's people need to be careful not to think they are better than others.

There was a wicked king and city that mistreated the people of Israel. God asked his prophet, Jonah, to go and deliver a message of repentance to the people of Nineveh. Jonah knew of the people in Nineveh and did not want to go to their city.

Instead he boarded a ship going in the opposite direction. Once on board, the ship faced trouble and Jonah identified himself as the reason for the trouble. The sailors threw him into the water and God commanded a big fish to swallow Jonah. While trapped in the belly of the fish, he prayed, asking God to forgive and save him. After three days, the fish vomited him out and Jonah went to Nineveh. Even when Jonah arrived he was suspicious of the people and wanted God to destroy them because of their wicked ways. In spite of Jonah's desires, the people listened to his warning, repented and feared God. God did not destroy them as he warned.

Observation: God loved the wicked nation regardless of their sin. His mercy extends to everyone. The purpose of Jonah is to show that God is free to demonstrate love and mercy to whomever He pleases. The most important theme of the book is that God rules over all nations. The book of Jonah demonstrates that God is ready to extend His mercy and grace beyond what is expected.

▶ **Question**: Can you share the love of Christ to someone that hates you or persecutes you?

▶ **Action Point**: Go and show love to someone that you do not think deserves love. Write their name down and go and do it!

Name: _____

Micah

The book of *Micah* says that God will bring judgment on anyone who mistreats others for personal gain. Micah calls God's people in both the northern and southern kingdoms to remember their need to live by His rules to stay in a right relationship with Him. If they did not, they would be judged. Micah means "Who is like the Lord?"

Micah contains one of the clearest prophecies about Jesus in the Old Testament. He predicted Jesus' birth in Bethlehem (*5:2*). Several themes are found in the book of *Micah*. One is that God's judgment is certain (*1:2-3:12*). God expected standards of behavior that fulfilled His laws (*6:6-8*). Yet, the people of Israel and Judah did not care about God's standards. They created ways to steal from others (*2:1-2*). The rulers led with injustice (*3; 7:2-4*). After judgment, God would restore His people (*4*), under the leadership of Jesus (*5:2-4*).

Nahum

The book of *Nahum* tells about God's judgment on Nineveh, the city that repented after hearing God's warnings through the prophet Jonah. God's prophet Nahum says that because Nineveh failed to continue in obedience to God, they would be destroyed by Babylon. Nahum means "comfort."

God previously used Nineveh as His tool of judgment to bring down the northern kingdom of Israel. The purpose of *Nahum* is to show that even if God uses a nation or person for His own purposes, that nation or person is still accountable to God to obey His will and ways. The book of *Nahum* uses questions (*1:6, 9*) to help people think through its content.

Observation: Maybe you see and experience social injustices. Perhaps the leaders in your community or region take advantage of you and your people. Corruption may be everywhere you look with no end in sight. Likely you wonder why God would allow such wicked people to come to power. Take heart and recognize that just as you will be accountable for your behavior, so will they.

Habakkuk

The book of *Habakkuk* tells about the days in Judah just before Babylon took the first group of exiles from Judah to Babylon. The book tells about the prophet Habakkuk's struggle with his own faith as he tries to understand how God could use a nation like Babylon to discipline His people. God's answers to Habakkuk's questions gives a greater faith to the prophet, and hope to His people. The purpose of the book of *Habakkuk* is to show that even when it seems that evil is powerful, God is all-powerful and will judge evil.

<u>Observation</u>: Habakkuk begins with doubt and confusion (1:12-2:1). He deals with the hard question of why wicked people sometimes gain power and success (1:2-4). God has not abandoned His position as Ruler of the universe when this happens. He is ready to judge those who commit evil (1:5-11; 2:1-4). God brings clear answers to respond to that doubt (2:2-20). The key to understanding the ways of God is to know that the just live by faith (2:4). God's people have to depend on God, not their own understanding. Even today, sometimes it seems that God's ways don't make sense. At those times, we must respond in faith and trust that God is doing the right thing for His glory and our good.

Zephaniah

Zephaniah tells about the day when God will judge the sin of Judah and the surrounding nations. Zephaniah's prophecies made it clear that God's judgment was coming, and tells God's people to repent. Their response would decide how soon God's judgment would come upon Judah. Zephaniah means "the Lord treasured."

The purpose of *Zephaniah* is to announce the coming day of the Lord because of God's judgment on the sin of Judah and the nations around it.

▶ **Action Point**: Write five ways you can be more like Christ.

-
-
-
-
-

Haggai

The book of *Haggai* is a collection of four short messages to encourage the Jews in Jerusalem to complete the rebuilding of the temple. Haggai's name means "festival."

There were many times in the history of God's people where they worshiped idols made of wood, silver or gold. But the book of *Haggai* tells that God's people were worshiping their own comfort more than they worshiped God (*Hag. 1:3-11*). It was a different kind of idol, but just as deadly. It is the kind of idol many people worship today. God's people must make God and His concerns their highest priority (*Mat. 6:24*). When we make that choice, He will provide everything we need and more (*Mat. 6:31-33*).

▶ **Question**: What is one message you can share to encourage those around you?

Zechariah

Zechariah contains hope and encouragement for the returned Jewish exiles in Jerusalem. Zechariah means "The Lord remembers." The purpose of *Zechariah* was to tell the Jews in Jerusalem to return to God, finish the temple, and to hope in the glorious future God had for them. *Zechariah* has many prophecies that Jesus fulfilled.

Zechariah's Prophecy	*Jesus' Fulfillment*
Messiah enters into Jerusalem on a colt (*Zec. 9:9*)	*Mat. 21:4-5* *Joh. 12:14-16*
Messiah betrayed for 30 pieces of silver (*Zec. 11:12-13*)	*Mat. 27:9, 10*
Messiah's hands and feet pierced (*Zec. 12:10*)	*Joh. 19:37*
Messiah's death cleanses from sin (*Zec. 13:1*)	*Joh. 1:29* *Tit. 3:5*
Messiah will reign in new Jerusalem (*Zec. 14:9, 16*)	*Rev. 20:4-6*
Messiah will serve as Priest-King (*Zec. 6:13*)	*Heb. 6:20-7:1*
Messiah is God's Shepherd (*Zec. 13:7*)	*Joh. 10:11-18*

Malachi

The book of *Malachi* shows what happens when God's people both forget His love for them, and live in rebellion. Over 70 years had passed since the second temple in Jerusalem had been dedicated. The temple should have been a place that celebrated God's presence among His people. Yet over time, worship in Jerusalem had become empty and dull. The people of God forgot God as they worshiped. As a result, they forgot His ways in everyday life.

Malachi means "My messenger." The purpose of *Malachi* was to call God's people to a new commitment and obedience in response to God's promises. The themes in *Malachi* tell about how important a person's heart and attitudes are in true worship. *Malachi* demands that everyone, from the priests to the people, should test their attitudes toward God and each other. *Malachi* says that the people do not care about God, and mistreat each other (*2:13-15*). God's people have forgotten His love for them (*1:2*). Malachi shows that the worship of God is not just a matter of the right ceremony or ritual, but also a matter of the right heart toward God.

God called Malachi to declare judgment on His people, and also to call them back to Him.

Assignment

Read and meditate on the verses below (*Malachi 1:6-14*):

> *The Lord of Heaven's Armies says to the priests: "A son honors his father, and a servant respects his master. If I am your father and master, where are the honor and respect I deserve? You have shown contempt for My name! "But you ask, 'How have we ever shown contempt for Your name?' "You have shown contempt by offering defiled sacrifices on My altar. "Then you ask, 'How have we defiled the sacrifices? "You defile them by saying the altar of the Lord deserves no respect. When you give blind animals as sacrifices, isn't that wrong? And isn't it wrong to offer animals that are crippled and diseased? Try giving gifts like that to your governor, and see how pleased He is!" says the Lord of Heaven's Armies. "Go ahead, beg God to*

be merciful to you! But when you bring that kind of offering, why should He show you any favor at all?" asks the Lord of Heaven's Armies.

"How I wish one of you would shut the Temple doors so that these worthless sacrifices could not be offered! I am not pleased with you," says the Lord of Heaven's Armies, "and I will not accept your offerings. But My name is honored by people of other nations from morning till night. All around the world they offer sweet incense and pure offerings in honor of My name. For My name is great among the nations," says the Lord of Heaven's Armies. "But you dishonor My name with your actions. By bringing contemptible food, you are saying it's all right to defile the Lord's table. You say, 'It's too hard to serve the Lord,' and you turn up your noses at My commands," says the Lord of Heaven's Armies. "Think of it! Animals that are stolen and crippled and sick are being presented as offerings! Should I accept from you such offerings as these?" asks the Lord. "Cursed is the cheat who promises to give a fine ram from his flock but then sacrifices a defective one to the Lord. For I am a great king," says the Lord of Heaven's Armies, "and My name is feared among the nations!"

Consider this Summary of the Old Testament

The Law
Genesis through Deuteronomy: All nations will be blessed through you.

God tells Abraham he will have a son, even though Abraham and his wife are old.

God says that through Abraham's descendants every nation on the earth will be blessed.

Jesus is a descendent of Abraham. He is the blessing to all nations.

History Books
One example: Ruth — Kinsman Redeemer

Ruth's husband dies

Someone from her husband's line redeems her and marries her, taking Ruth under his protection.

Similarly, Jesus is our Kinsman Redeemer.

Poetry Books:
"They divide my garments among themselves and throw dice for my clothing."
(*Psalms 22:18*)

"They divide my garments among themselves..."

... and throw dice for my clothing."

During the crucifixion the soldiers ripped Jesus' garments and cast lots. (*John 19:23-24*)

Prophets:
"The Lord himself will give you the sign. Look! The virgin will conceive a child! She will give birth to a son and will call him Immanuel (which means 'God with us.')"
(*Psalms 22:18*)

"The Lord himself will give you the sign. Look! The virgin will conceive a child!"

"She will give birth to a son and will call him Immanuel."

Jesus is conceived of the Holy Spirit, born of the virgin Mary. (*Matthew 1:18*)

Chapter 5
New Testament Gospels

The Gospels are the first four books of the New Testament - Matthew, Mark, Luke, and John. Each is named after its author. The word Gospel means "Good News."

The four Gospels focus on the life and ministry of Jesus Christ and teach the power of God that brought salvation (It is the story of the life, death, and resurrection of Jesus Christ). They focus on key events and teachings in the life of Jesus. The Gospels are history with a purpose.

> *The disciples saw Jesus do many other miraculous signs in addition to the ones recorded in this book. But these are written so that you may continue to believe that Jesus is the Messiah, the Son of God, and that by believing in Him you will have life by the power of His name. (John 20:30-31).*

Observation: What is revealed in the Gospels about Jesus is enough to believe in Him and receive salvation.

Each Gospel is unique:

1. **Matthew**: was a Tax Collector and disciple of Jesus.

2. **Mark**: was a missionary with Barnabas and Paul (see *Acts 12:12,25; 13:5-13; 15:36-39*).

3. **Luke**: was a Greek medical doctor and historian who traveled with the Apostle Paul. Luke also wrote the Book of Acts.

4. **John**: was a fisherman and a disciple of Jesus.

Observation: The Gospels are not legends or myths. They are factual accounts written while many eyewitnesses were still living. If the accounts had been in error, those eyewitnesses would have objected.

But why four Gospels? Wouldn't one be good enough? There are at least three reasons why God decided to put four Gospels in the Bible:

1. **To Proclaim Truth**. The Bible says, *"Everything you say may be confirmed by two or three witnesses"* (*Matthew 18:16*). With the Gospels we have more than two or three witnesses... we have four!

2. **To Clearly Show God's Glory**. The Gospel of John says about Jesus, *"So the Word became human and made His home among us. He was full of unfailing love and faithfulness. And we have seen His glory, the glory of the Father's one and only Son"* (*John 1:14*). The four Gospels reveal different aspects of the glory of God shown to us in Jesus.

3. **To Show Jesus to All People, in All Cultures (both Jews and Gentiles)**. The Bible says, *"For God loved the world so much that he gave His one and only Son, so that everyone who believes in Him will not perish but have eternal life"* (*John 3:16*).

God wants the Gospel shared with everyone in the world!

Matthew: The Gospel of the King

Before becoming a follower of Jesus, Matthew collected taxes for the Romans. This type of job would have made Matthew offensive to his own people, the Jews. After his conversion, Matthew became a disciple of Jesus. In his Gospel, Matthew shows Jesus as the Messiah and King.

There are at least four clear purposes of the Gospel of Matthew:

1. **To prove to the Jews that Jesus is the Messiah**. For example, the genealogy of Jesus in chapter one proves that Jesus descended from King David.

2. **To describe the Kingdom of God**. The Gospels many references to the Kingdom show that it is revealed in Jesus, even though Jesus does not yet physically rule on earth.

3. **To explain the beginning of the Church**. This is the only Gospel to refer to the Church (Matthew 16:18; 18:17).

4. **To show Jesus as a Teacher**. The Gospel of Matthew focuses on Jesus' words. It has five major collections of Jesus' teachings:

   • The Sermon on the Mount (*Matthew 5-7*)

   • Warning about Opposition (*Matthew 10*)

   • Parables about the Kingdom (*Matthew 13*)

   • Parables and Teachings about Humility (*Matthew 18*)

   • The End Times (*Matthew 23-25*)

Mark: The Gospel of the Servant

Mark was a disciple of Jesus. Mark's Gospel is described as a short version of Jesus' life and ministry.

There are at least three clear purposes:

1. **To maintain the facts about Jesus**. As the time of the eyewitness accounts grew farther apart, Mark understood the importance of writing down the stories of Jesus' words and deeds.

2. **To encourage worried believers**. Mark wrote at a time when Roman Christians were beginning to experience persecution. His description of a Savior who overcame mistreatment and even murder would have given them courage.

3. **To show and emphasize the miracles of Jesus**. *Mark* is a book of action!

Luke: The Gospel of the Son of Man

Luke was a Greek medical doctor, and a disciple of Jesus. Luke wrote both his Gospel and the *Book of Acts*. This Gospel is clearly written from a non-Jewish point of view.

There are at least two clear purposes for the writing of Luke's Gospel:

1. **To establish a strong historical foundation for the Gospel**. Luke himself said, *"Many people have set out to write accounts about the events that have been fulfilled among us. They used the eyewitness reports circulating among us from the early disciples. Having carefully investigated everything from the beginning, I also have decided to write a careful account for you, most honorable Theophilus, so you can be certain of the truth of everything you were taught (Luke 1:1-4).*

2. **To defend Christianity against its enemies**. At the time Luke wrote, Christianity was receiving criticism from the Jewish community and from some parts of the Gentile (any non-Jewish person is considered a Gentile) world, including Rome.

John: The Gospel of the Son of God

Jesus called John and his brother James to be His disciples (*Matthew 4:21; Luke 5:1-11*). Along with Peter and James, John became one of the three disciples who were closest to Jesus. John outlived all the other disciples and authored, by inspiration of the Holy Spirit, *1, 2, 3 John* and the *Book of Revelation*.

There are two clear purposes why John wrote this Gospel:

1. **To establish that Jesus was God in the form of Man**. John described Jesus as the "Word" who became a man (*John 1:1, 14*). John records the eight "I Am" statements of Jesus. The use of the words "I Am" by Jesus reflects the name that God gave to describe himself to Moses (*Exodus 3:14*). John's Gospel focuses on the close connection between the Father and the Son.

2. **To encourage all to trust in Jesus for Eternal Life**. The Gospel says, "*The disciples saw Jesus do many other miraculous signs in addition to the ones recorded in this book. But these are written so that you may continue to believe that Jesus is the Messiah, the Son of God, and that by believing in Him you will have life by the power of His name*" (*John 20:30-31*).

Assignment

How many disciples did Jesus have? Can you give the names? (See *Mt. 10:2-4, Mark 3:16-19, Luke 6:13-16*)

Introduction To The Life of Jesus

Since Adam and Eve sinned in the Garden of Eden, the human race needed a Savior. God gave the Israelites a system of laws and sacrifices, but none of that really saved them. It all just led to God's final solution to the problem of sin: Jesus!

God sent His own Son to come to earth as a man. For about three or four years Jesus modeled a public ministry. He taught people how to know God and demonstrated God's power and love towards them. Jesus died on the cross to pay the penalty for our sin. He made it possible for everyone to have a proper relationship with God if they believe in Him. Rising from the dead, He made it possible for a sinner to have eternal life and rule with God in His Kingdom forever.

Jesus' Preparation For Ministry

The birth of Jesus was prophesied by multiple prophets in the Old Testament (see charts in Chapter 4 of this book). Although the birth was ordinary in some ways, it was also supernatural. Jesus was conceived by the Holy Spirit and born of the virgin Mary (*Mt. 1:18-20*). His virgin birth was the beginning of a new phase of God's dealings with the human race.

The childhood of Jesus is not well known. The Scriptures intentionally give us little information about His childhood since what we need to know about Jesus was accomplished when He was an adult. We do know that Luke records the story of when Jesus was brought to Jerusalem for one of the important feast days. On their return trip, Mary and Joseph realized that Jesus was not with them. When they found Jesus, then just twelve years old, He was talking with the teachers in the Temple and amazing them. Jesus' divine wisdom and sense of special connection to God the Father were already evident.

When Jesus reached adulthood He probably followed in Joseph's profession as a carpenter in Nazareth. Then, about AD 29, He started His public ministry, around the age of thirty.

> *One day, Jesus approached a prophet named John the Baptist (who was baptizing people), requesting that he baptize Him*

(John was known as John the Baptizer and was sent for the purpose of announcing the coming of Jesus as the Messiah). John recognized who Jesus was and said, "You should baptize me!" Jesus convinced John that it was fulfilling God's plan, so John agreed. As John baptized Jesus the Holy Spirit came in the form of a dove and a declaration came from Heaven, saying, "This is my Son, in whom I am well pleased." (See Mt. 3:13-17)

Observation: Jesus set an example for us to follow. Baptism is a public declaration of our faith and association with Jesus. It is identifying with His death, burial and resurrection. Before He preached a sermon or worked a miracle He was first baptized. Jesus' baptism introduced Him and His ministry to Israel. When you are baptized you are likewise introducing yourself to those around you as a follower of Christ. It is the first act of obedience for a new believer.

▶ **Question**: Are you baptized?

▶ **Action Point**: If not, you should be! Follow the example of Jesus.

The ministry of Jesus officially started when John baptized Him. The Holy Spirit then led Jesus into the wilderness. Jesus spent forty days and nights fasting. At His weakest point physically Jesus demonstrated His spiritual strength by resisting the temptations of Satan.

Observation: After forty days of fasting Jesus was naturally hungry. However, this weakness and hunger did not push Him to dishonor His Father. Jesus was able to resist the Devil's temptations because He was in deep communion with His Father. You can resist Satan the same way.

The preparation and beginning of Jesus' public ministry concludes with the calling of some of His disciples (including some fishermen, a tax collector etc.) and His first recorded miracle... turning water into wine at a wedding *(John 2:1-12)*.

Jesus' First Year of Ministry: The Beginning of the Work

With His time of preparation over, Jesus began His first full year of ministry. We see Him participating in a variety of relationships, teaching interested people important spiritual truths, confronting the sinful, leading people into the service of God, and opposing evil in its many forms.

Jesus spent most of this first year in Judea, by the Jordan River, until after John the Baptist was put in prison. He experienced His first rejection in His hometown, Nazareth, in Galilee. From there He proceeded to the region around Capernaum, located in Galilee, where He chose most of His disciples.

The brevity of the Gospel writers concerning Jesus' first year of ministry may seem strange. Matthew, Mark, and Luke skip over most of this time, and even John only covers a small amount. It should be noted that it seems the disciples were not with Jesus during most of this time. It was not a period of inactivity, however. Jesus traveled throughout Galilee teaching, preaching, and healing. He was often followed by large numbers of people.

By the end of Jesus' first year of public ministry there must have been a feeling in Galilee, if not in all of Palestine, that something big was happening. Word spread quickly that a miracle worker had appeared. He had amazing things to say about God as well. Who was this man? What was He going to do for the nation? With such a beginning, Jesus' ministry was about to enter its period of greatest popularity. One story from this period describes the interaction between Jesus and a religious leader.

One day, Jesus was teaching religious leaders in a house. His reputation was growing as a great healer. Four men heard Him speaking and remembered their paralyzed friend. When they brought their friend to the house where Jesus was speaking, it was too crowded to go inside. The men climbed up onto the roof, made a hole in it and lowered their friend down in his bed.
Seeing their faith, Jesus turned His attention to the paralyzed man. Jesus told the man, "Take heart my son, your sins are forgiven." Some of the religious leaders there questioned how Jesus could say such a thing. After all, who can forgive sins but God alone? Jesus responded to their thoughts and said, "Which

is easier, to say your sins are forgiven or rise and walk?" But so that they would know that the Son of Man has authority on earth, He said, "Rise, pick up your mattress and go home." Instantly the paralyzed man stood up and was healed! When the crowd saw this act of power, they praised God and marveled at Jesus, saying they had never seen anything like this before. (Mt. 9:1-8; Mar. 2:1-12; Luke 5:17-26)

Use the SWORD method of interpretation and application to answer the questions below:

1. What do we learn about God?

    •

    •

2. What do we learn about Man?

    •

    •

3. What principles do we learn, or what sins should we avoid?

    •

    •

4. What commands are there to obey, or examples to follow?

    •

    •

5. What is my response? What must I do? Action Points:

    •

    •

Jesus' Second Year of Ministry: A Time of Popularity

Starting His second year of ministry, Jesus faced challenges from the religious leaders. These leaders thought He violated their rules about what could and couldn't be done on the Sabbath, the weekly Jewish holy day.

Jesus' second year of ministry was a period of activity and wide public acceptance. It was also a time of conflict with the religious leaders, causing more of their disapproval. An important event during that second year was Jesus' "Sermon on the Mount." This was given not as a way of salvation, but to clarify forever the true nature of righteousness and God's Kingdom. Jesus confirmed the prophet Micah's emphasis - that God desires justice, kindness, and walking humbly with Him - and He clearly showed the difference between true heart-righteousness from rituals and religion. This message caused much difficulty to the Pharisees and religious leaders, because Jesus was rejecting their entire system.

After that sermon Jesus traveled around Galilee, performing many miracles to display Himself as Son of God. The religious leaders tried to explain these miracles as Satan-inspired. Responding to this serious charge, Jesus began using parables in His teaching. He turned away from those rejecting Him and focused on the people that were willing to listen. During this time, John the Baptist was killed. Shortly afterward, Jesus miraculously fed a crowd of thousands and gained so much approval that the people wanted to make Him king. Yet, it was soon clear that the people did not want to follow Jesus as their king.

What extraordinary things our Lord could do! When God walked among human beings He healed, taught and did amazing works!

All this drew much attention to Jesus. From early in His ministry He encountered challenges from the religious leaders that felt threatened by Him. These challenges only increased. Soon there came a decrease in Jesus' popularity among the people, due to the religious leader's opposition. This would lead Him closer to His greatest work of all, ***His sacrifice on the cross***. Consider and discuss one story from this period.

> *One day, Jesus preached to a large crowd of people. As time passed, many people were hungry. The disciples approached Jesus, requesting that He send them away to eat. Jesus responded by asking them, "Why don't you feed them?" They were unable to do this, of course. Andrew, one of Jesus' disciples, brought*

one boy with five loaves of bread and two fish. Jesus had the disciples divide the crowd into groups of 50 and then sit down. Jesus took the bread and fish, blessed it, and gave it to the disciples to distribute to the crowd of 5,000 men. The entire crowd ate their full and when they were finished, there were 12 baskets leftover. (See *Matthew 14:13-21* for the whole story)

1. What do we learn about God?
   -
   -

2. What do we learn about Man?
   -
   -

3. What principles do we learn, or what sins should we avoid?
   -
   -

4. What commands are there to obey, or examples to follow?
   -
   -

5. What is my response? What must I do? Action Points:
   -
   -

Jesus' Third Year of Ministry: A Time of Rejection

During Jesus' third year of ministry things became more difficult. The religious leaders were more determined to persecute Him. Meanwhile, some of the ordinary people turned against Him as well. None of this stopped Jesus, but it did lead Him to make changes in His ministry.

<u>Observation</u>: Notice that when Jesus faced difficulty He did not stop His work…He made changes in order to fulfill the task He had been given.

▶ **Question**: What is the task you have been given as a disciple?

"He came to his own people, and even they rejected him." (*John 1:11*) Jesus would not force Himself on anyone. Whenever He was rejected in one place, He went on to the next place. With so much rejection, to whom would He go next?

Twice Jesus escaped death in Jerusalem during His third year of ministry. His time had not yet come…but it would soon. And He knew it. He spoke clearly with His disciples about His upcoming death at the hands of the religious leaders. In the final year of Jesus' ministry, it was clear that Jesus was committed to fulfill His Father's plan of providing salvation for all mankind for all ages. Consider and discuss the following story told by Jesus: (*John 10:1-21*)

> *"I tell you the truth, anyone who sneaks over the wall of a sheepfold, rather than going through the gate, must surely be a thief and a robber! But the One who enters through the gate is the shepherd of the sheep. The gatekeeper opens the gate for Him, and the sheep recognize His voice and come to Him. He calls His own sheep by name and leads them out. After He has gathered His own flock, He walks ahead of them, and they follow Him because they know His voice. They won't follow a stranger; they will run from Him because they don't know His voice."* Those who heard Jesus use this illustration didn't understand what He meant, so He explained it to them: *"I tell you the truth, I am the gate for the sheep. All who came before Me were thieves and robbers. But the true sheep did not listen to them. Yes, I am the gate. Those who come in through Me will be saved. They will*

come and go freely and will find good pastures. The thief's purpose is to steal and kill and destroy. My purpose is to give them a rich and satisfying life. "I am the good shepherd. The good shepherd sacrifices His life for the sheep. A hired hand will run when he sees a wolf coming. He will abandon the sheep because they don't belong to him and he isn't their shepherd. And so the wolf attacks them and scatters the flock. The hired hand runs away because he's working only for the money and doesn't really care about the sheep. "I am the good shepherd; I know My own sheep, and they know Me, just as my Father knows Me and I know the Father. So I sacrifice My life for the sheep. I have other sheep, too, that are not in this sheepfold. I must bring them also. They will listen to My voice, and there will be one flock with one shepherd. "The Father loves Me because I sacrifice my life so I may take it back again. No one can take My life from me. I sacrifice it voluntarily. For I have the authority to lay it down when I want to and also to take it up again. For this is what My Father has commanded. "When He said these things, the people were again divided in their opinions about Him. Some said, "He's demon possessed and out of His mind. Why listen to a man like that?" Others said, "This doesn't sound like a man possessed by a demon! Can a demon open the eyes of the blind?"

Use the SWORD method of interpretation and application and answer the following questions:

1. What do we learn about God?

    •

    •

    •

2. What do we learn about Man?

    •

    •

    •

3. What principles do we learn, or what sins should we avoid?

-

-

-

4. What commands are there to obey, or examples to follow?

-

-

-

5. What is my response? What must I do? Action Points:

-

-

Jesus' Fourth Year of Ministry: Heading Toward the Cross

The story of Jesus' fourth year of ministry is one of heading toward Jerusalem and the cross. Over the course of the year, He prepared His followers for what was going to happen and began finishing up His public ministry.

Jesus headed for Jerusalem to meet His death. The entire time He instructed His disciples, challenged the crowds, invited them to follow Him, and challenged the religious leadership. He prepared the disciples for what would happen in the near future and the ministry they would serve after He was gone. Jesus gave the crowds more opportunities to respond. He showed that the way of the current religious leaders was not the way of God. In this section we get the clearest understanding of His teaching during a time of great opposition.

Jesus focused on preparing His disciples for what would soon happen. By February of AD 33, Jesus was not far from Jerusalem, in Jericho. From Jericho, where Jesus healed a blind man and led a tax collector to faith, Jesus departed for Jerusalem. He chose the time of Passover (a Jewish festival celebrating their deliverance from Egypt) to make His entry into the city and face the final week of His life.

While Jesus was busy teaching in one place, the disciples received word that their friend Lazarus was very sick and requested that Jesus come to him. Jesus did not go immediately, but waited two days. Jesus said to the disciples, "It is good for you that we were not there so that the Son of God may be glorified before you." When they arrived Lazarus' sisters ran to Jesus and told Him that Lazarus had died. They said, "If only You had come, Lazarus would not have died." Jesus said that Lazarus was not dead, but was sleeping. Jesus then requested that they go to the place he was buried. Jesus wept and the people said, "Look at how much He loved him!" Jesus told them to remove the stone from the grave. Although the people warned Him that it would smell, Jesus assured them that it was okay. Jesus prayed, gave thanks to the Father, and said "Lazarus, come out" Immediately, Lazarus came out of the tomb! The people were amazed, for the man that was dead was alive and came out! (See John 11:1-44 for the whole story)

Use the SWORD method of interpretation and application and answer the questions below:

1. What do we learn about God?

   •

   •

   •

2. What do we learn about Man?

   •

   •

3. What principles do we learn, or what sins should we avoid?

    •

    •

4. What commands are there to obey, or examples to follow?

    •

    •

    •

5. What is my response? What must I do? Action Points:

    •

    •

Jesus' Final Week: The Work of Redemption Started

The term "Passion" is used to describe Jesus' sufferings and death. It is no surprise that each of the Gospels gives more attention to the Passion than to any other part of Jesus' story. This is where Jesus fulfilled His mission. This is where He completed the work of salvation for all who believe. This is where He is proved victorious over sin, Satan, death and the grave.

The Passion took place within the space of about a week. The following is a short summary of the week of Passion:

Sunday	Jesus enters Jerusalem with rejoicing (Palm Sunday)
Monday	Jesus curses a fig tree & cleanses the Temple
Tuesday	Jesus' authority is questioned and He teaches in the Temple
Wednesday	Jesus' enemies plot against Him

Thursday	Jesus shares the Last Supper with His disciples and prays at Gethsemane
Friday	Jesus is betrayed, arrested, tried, crucified and buried
Saturday	Jesus' body remains in the tomb
Sunday	Jesus rises from the dead!

Below is the most wonderful story ever told! Read or listen to this carefully, commit it to memory and share with all you know!

As Jesus came to his last week of earthly ministry He entered Jerusalem. On Thursday night Jesus and the disciples gathered in an upper room. Jesus wanted to tell the disciples what was about to happen, as this would be their last time together. During the meal Jesus washed the feet of each of His disciples. This was a common practice for servants to wash the feet of a guest, but never by a master and leader. After He finished washing their feet, they had a meal together. During the meal Jesus took bread, blessed it, and gave it to the disciples saying, "Take, eat, this is My body which is given for you." He also took a cup of wine and when He had given thanks said, "Drink of it, all of you, for this is my blood, the covenant which is poured out for many; do this in remembrance of me." Though the disciples did not understand what this meal represented, it was a significant event that was the beginning of the Lord's Supper (See John 13:1-17 and Luke 22:7-20 for the whole story).

After dinner they walked to a nearby garden. Jesus asked the disciples to join Him in prayer as He was troubled and anticipated His coming death. Some of the religious leaders had already been plotting to kill Him. They had a secret plan with one of Jesus' disciples called Judas Iscariot. Judas Iscariot brought the religious leaders and guards to arrest Jesus. The disciples scattered in fear and Jesus was arrested and taken to the house of the High Priest. He was mocked and ridiculed. He was taken to different political leaders but they could not find any fault in Him. Even the governor said "This man has done nothing wrong."

As the news of Jesus' arrest spread, the crowds grew around the place where Jesus was held. The religious leaders enticed the crowds and encouraged them to demand that Jesus be crucified. Due to the pressure from the crowds, the governor (named Pilate) was forced to declare Jesus would be crucified. The guards stripped Him, beat Him, whipped Him, spit on Him, mocked Him, and made Him carry a cross through the city to the place where He would be crucified.

Jesus was taken to a place called Golgotha and was crucified between two criminals. They drove two nails into His hands and one nail between His feet to hold Him to the cross. As Jesus was on the cross He asked the Father to forgive the people who were killing Him. Finally, Jesus gave up His life, breathed His last breath and died. One soldier came and pierced His side to make sure He was really dead; and then He was buried in a new tomb according to what was prophesied about Him.

The religious leaders asked to seal the tomb where Jesus was buried, as Jesus had predicted His resurrection earlier. They also posted guards at the tomb to make sure that no one attempted to steal His body. Early Sunday morning, three days after Jesus was crucified, a powerful earthquake took place. The stone was removed and Jesus resurrected from the dead! He then appeared to His disciples and other followers for many days. He encouraged them to be witnesses of what they had seen, heard, and to tell others! Finally, in the presence of many followers, he ascended to Heaven and promised to return the same way. Just before leaving them He told the disciples to wait in Jerusalem until He sent His Holy Spirit to empower them for the task ahead of them! (See *Matthew 26-28* and *Luke 24* for the complete story)

Jesus' Work Completed

We have reached the end of the Life of Christ on earth. Many Old Testament prophecies have been fulfilled, beginning with the first prophecy in *Genesis 3:15*: *The serpent's offspring would strike the heel of the woman's offspring, and the serpent's head would be crushed.* The final crushing of Satan will include the destruction of his kingdom of darkness and the establishment on earth of God's Kingdom of righteousness.

All prophecy revolves around Jesus, His life, death and resurrection. It was through His death and resurrection that Christ fulfilled His commission from the Father: to provide a way of redemption for mankind and to reclaim God's Kingdom and authority everywhere.

Christ is still fulfilling His mission. He offers freedom from sin and death to all who by faith receive Him as their personal Savior. Entering God's Kingdom comes only by spiritual birth, a work of the Holy Spirit, as one receives this gift of God's Son (*John 3*).

The resurrection means not only that Jesus is alive and that there is life after death, but also that He is shown to be who He claimed to be. God the Father has exalted Jesus into His presence in Heaven. On the day of Pentecost, God poured out His Holy Spirit upon all who believe in Jesus. The Holy Spirit is now the companion, comforter and guide for all believers today.

Jesus reigns this very day in Heaven. It is Jesus, the risen and exalted Savior that the four Gospels tell all about. It is this Jesus, that we worship and proclaim to the world.

▸ **Question**: How can you keep this wonderful story all to yourself? Can you keep quiet about this story? No! You must share it with others!

▸ **Action Point**: Write down ten names that you can go and share this story with:

1.   6.

2.   7.

3.   8.

4.   9.

5.   10.

Read at least one of the four Gospels in the New Testament this week. Write down in your own words the story of the Gospel.

_____

_____

_____

_____

_____

_____

_____

_____

_____

_____

_____

_____

_____

_____

_____

_____

_____

_____

_____

Consider this Summary of the Life of Jesus

An angel told Mary that, by the Power of the Holy Spirit, she would conceive a son.

She would name Him Jesus, and He would be the Son of God.

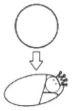

When Jesus grew up, He started His ministry.

He was baptized.

He called disciples to join Him.

He performed miracles like healing the sick.

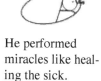

Raising the dead...

He taught people about His Father.

It seemed like everyone loved Jesus...

But some people did not. They wanted Jesus to die.

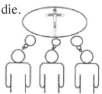

They falsely accused Him.

He was crucified, and He died.

He was buried.

After three days He rose from the dead!

He appeared to His disciples and many others.

He told His disciples to tell everyone His story.

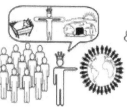

He ascended into Heaven.

He will return to take those who believe to be with Him.

Consider this Story (Luke 15:11-32)

A man had two sons.

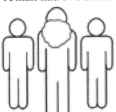

One son asked for his inheritance early.

He wasted it.

He was left in poverty.

He decided to return home.

His father was waiting for him.

The father ran to him.

He gave him new clothes and had a celebration.

His oldest son was mad at His father's response.

God is:

Love

Grace

Forgiveness

Restoration

Teaches us about man's...

Sinfulness

Rebellion

Repentance

Pride

Consider this Story (John 4:1-42)

There were two groups of people who did not like each other: the Jews and the Samaritans.

Jesus was traveling through Samaria.

He was tired, and he asked a woman for a drink.

She was confused because Jews did not talk to Samaritans.

Jesus says He gives water that will make her never thirst again.

She asks for that water.

Jesus asks her to call for her husband.

She says she has no husband.

Jesus says that she has had five husbands, and the man she is with now is not her husband.

Jesus reveals Himself as Messiah.

The woman is amazed by what He knew and tells her village. Many believe and follow Jesus.

Chapter 6
General Letters
of the New Testament

History tells us that Roman rule changed the world. Roads throughout the empire made travel easier than ever before. Culture, philosophies and religions met in the cities along these roads. The Jewish people were only one of many ethnic groups the Romans governed. This is the situation in which Jesus Christ was born, the Church was raised up and books of the New Testament were written.

The New Testament has four different kinds of writings:

- **Gospels** — *Matthew, Mark, Luke* and *John* record the life of Christ (See Chapter 5).

- *Acts* — This book tells the story of the early church and the spread of the Gospel (See Chapter 3).

- **Letters** — New Testament's letters are divided into two: Paul's letters and general letters. Paul's letters are the ones written by Paul and his team members. General letters are the ones written by other church leaders. Most of these letters were written to individual churches or leaders across the growing New Testament Church.

- **Vision** — The book of Revelation stands alone in the New Testament. In this book there are many visions, symbols and images that picture God's actions in the time to come.

Romans

Paul is the writer of this letter to the church in Rome. He wrote it while he was in Corinth around AD 57. Paul had not visited Rome before writing this letter to them. It is very important to know that the church in Rome was not planted by any Apostle. Some of the people who were in Jerusalem on the day of Pentecost, went back to Rome with the Gospel of Jesus and planted this church. This should encourage you that every disciple of Christ, **even you, can plant a church**! Paul used this letter to give a strong foundation for the Christian doctrine of salvation.

Consider the following story: *There was a man named Kofi, born into a religious family that recognized there was a Supreme God. Kofi was raised to think that if he did well he would not offend the Supreme God, but if he did bad he would offend this God. Regardless, there was no relationship there and Kofi did not have any interest in this God. He turned away from this God he was introduced to as a child and lived life for himself. After some time Kofi became very sick (loss of weight, appetite, strength and felt miserable) and went to the traditional local hospitals. They could not determine what his sickness was. As a result, he was advised to go to the local witch doctor to be healed. On his visit to the witch doctor he was told that there were people who wanted to kill him. Kofi was told that if he worshiped the thunder god those wanting to kill him would die and he would be protected.*

Kofi became a thunder god disciple, but the problem and sickness did not go away. Kofi was directed towards another god; this time a destroyer god, who would kill someone in his place. The priests carried Kofi to a cemetery at night, dug a grave and Kofi lied down inside. They placed medicine on his body and preformed ceremonies and incantations. They promised that someone would die in Kofi's place. When they finished, they let him out and Kofi returned to the house and took a holy bath. The sickness only got worse. Kofi went to a third witch doctor and worshiped the god of health. There he received a list of things to buy and take for medication. On his way to buy the medicine, somehow Kofi heard an inner voice saying, "You are having all these problems, but what will happen when you die and have to face the Supreme God?" The next four to five days Kofi was unable to sleep. It was clear to Kofi that he was dying as he had lost more than 20 kgs and his body was even beginning to stink.

On his deathbed, Kofi acknowledged the voice he was hearing. He promised to remove all the connections to the different gods he worshiped and removed all the idols from his house. After he removed all these things, he kneeled down in his room and prayed to God saying, "If I must die I am ready" but asked that he be saved. After this, Kofi fell asleep for a long time. When he woke up the next day, he was fully healed! He could not believe what happened. He knew something happened but did not know what it was. He decided to go to a church so he prayed, asking God which one he should attend. On the way, he met an old friend who took him to a church. Kofi heard that a life with Jesus made him more than a conqueror. When the preacher was preaching it was clear to Kofi that this was the true Supreme God. Kofi learned that there was nothing that he could do in his own power. It was only Jesus who had the power to save his body from his sickness and save his spirit from the gods. After the message the pastor asked who would like to give their life to Jesus. Kofi declared that he wanted to live his life for Jesus from that day forward. Kofi came to learn that this salvation was offered as a free gift from God. It was not by his rituals, efforts, money, obedience or knowledge. It was only by faith in the life, death, and resurrection of Jesus Christ.

After that day, Kofi was baptized and quickly decided to serve Jesus the rest of his life. He is confident that his safety and salvation are secure in the Lord, by the power of Jesus. Nothing can take this away from him. His mother, brother and other family members are following Jesus to this day as a result of his testimony and teaching of the Scriptures.

<u>Observation</u>: Based on the book of *Romans* and Kofi's story we learn that mankind is separated from God as a result of their sin. All human efforts and attempts to earn anything from God are useless. Salvation is only available in Jesus by His grace, through faith in Him and His promises. We cannot buy, earn, or take it. It is freely given.

▶ **Action Point**: Write your story of salvation today! Focus on the work of Christ in your life and what He has done for you.

_____

_____

_____

_____

_____

_____

_____

1 Corinthians

Corinth was a commercial and multicultural town. Philosophies and religions mixed freely. The worship of idols promoted prostitution in the name of religion. The city became famous for immorality. Paul and his team planted the church in Corinth and stayed there for about a year and half (read *Acts 18:1–18*). While the church was growing, division and immorality came. The members were even using their spiritual gifts against the will of God. Pride took over where humility once existed. Paul wrote this letter to solve the conflicts in the church and to answer many questions the Corinthians had asked him.

2 Corinthians

Paul made a visit to Corinth. He describes the visit as "painful" (*2 Cor. 2:1*). In between his visit and writing of *2 Corinthians* Paul received word that the church in Corinth was responding well. Paul then wrote *2 Corinthians* to express his joy. He also defended his authority as an apostle.

We continue with Kofi's Story: *As Kofi began to grow in the Lord as a new believer, he wanted to go to church. The church he decided to attend made it clear to him that he must show evidence of certain gifts from the Holy Spirit. The problem was Kofi did not possess all of these gifts. Even after fasting for 3 days, nothing changed. He became discouraged, felt unspiritual and useless. Kofi searched the Scriptures and came across 2 Corinthians 3:17 which says, "For the Lord is the Spirit, and wherever the Spirit of the Lord is, there is freedom." This verse helped him realize that if he has Jesus, he already has the Holy Spirit. He is free from having to show any special signs of salvation.*

Observation: As believers, the Bible tells us that that the Holy Spirit gives gifts to all. We have to be aware that the Holy Spirit gives different gifts to each one, as He pleases, for the glory of God and encouraging the Church. The greatest gift of all is love! (*Rom 5:5; 1 Cor. 13*)

- *1 Cor. 12:7*—A spiritual gift is given to all believers for the purpose of helping each other and glorifying God.
- *1 Cor. 12:11*—It is the one and only Spirit who distributes all these gifts. He alone decides which gifts each person should have.

▶ **Action Point**: Write down some observations below.

_____

_____

_____

_____

_____

_____

_____

Galatians

The region of Galatia is now called Turkey. Paul and his team planted churches in cities of the Galatian region. The Galatians opened their hearts to the Gospel that Paul preached and they believed that they were saved by grace, live every day by grace and will live forever in His grace. Some false teachers came to the churches and introduced false teaching. They taught that people first must follow the Law of Moses; only then could they become believers in Christ. Many Galatians were deceived and followed these false teachers. Paul's letter to the Galatians corrects the false teachers and clarifies again that God saves us by His grace. We do not earn salvation by following rules or good works. We are saved by grace, we live every day by grace and will live forever in His grace. All is by our Lord's pure grace.

We continue with Kofi's story: *As a new believer, Kofi attempted to earn God's favor. For one year he didn't miss church or forget to tithe. He fasted and prayed in order to ensure God was pleased with him. He thought that by doing these things he would make God happy. If he did things for God, he thought God would do things for him. On the day of his baptism Kofi's friend told him that from then on he would have to be very careful not to make God angry. Kofi was very nervous and uncomfortable in his faith until he discovered that his actions and works are not what pleases God. It is his faith and hope in Christ that save him, not his works. He realized that faith in action pleases God.*

Observation: It is important to remember that we are saved by grace, we live every day by grace, and will live forever in God's grace. Any system of works or duties cannot earn any favor with God. As we grow in Christ, as noted by Kofi above, we must walk with Jesus by faith and not by sight. We are rewarded as Christians for the fruit that we bear through living in faith. Spiritual works are the evidence, not the energizer of sincere faith.

> ▶ **Action Point**: One of the ways we can evaluate the work of the Holy Spirit in our lives is by the fruit that is produced. Read the following verses and note down all you observe about what the Holy Spirit of God will produce in you.
>
> *But the Holy Spirit produces this kind of fruit in our lives: love, joy, peace, patience, kindness, goodness, faithfulness, gentleness, and self-control. There is no law against these things! Those who belong to Christ Jesus have nailed the passions and desires of their sinful nature to His cross and crucified them there. Since we are living by the Spirit, let us follow the Spirit's leading in every part of our lives. Let us not become conceited, or provoke one another, or be jealous of one another* (Galatians 5:22-26).

What does the Holy Spirit produce in you?

-
-
-
-
-
-
-
-
-

Ephesians

Paul stayed in a city called Ephesus for three years during his second missionary journey. He planted the first church in this city and later wrote a letter to the churches that came out of his first church. A church by its essence must be missions-minded and look to reproduce itself. The first half of the letter talks about key beliefs of the Christian faith and our privileges. The second half describes how beliefs turn into actions. Paul was in prison when he wrote the letter to the Ephesians around AD 60.

Observation: There must be unity and sharing in the local church. The role of the leadership in the church is to equip the believers for the work of the ministry. One person may be the leader, but he is to share the workload and equip other leaders (4:1-16).

Observation: In some places, tribes or people groups are identified by scars on their faces. These markings can also signify a relationship with a certain god. There is a strong desire to be identified to a tribe, people or god. Some people wear pictures of their gods on their jewelry. Others wear particular clothes as indication of a certain god they worship.

Some people shave their head, mark their forehead or body with special religious symbols. All of this is to help identify themselves with something bigger and greater than themselves.

▶ **Question**: As a Christian, where do you find your identity?

▶ **Action Point**: Read these verses from *Ephesians*. Write down what each verse tells about our identity in Christ.

1:3

1:4

1:5-6

1:7

2:6

2:10

2:13

3:6

3:12

Philippians

Philippi was the leading city in Greece (*Acts 16:6-12*). Paul and his team planted a church in that city. Philippi was a multicultural city, and viewed the church as a mixture of people from different races and cultures. The first person to believe was a wealthy woman named Lydia and the church met in her house (*Acts 16:14-15*). Paul was in prison at that time, but he wrote about great joy and partnership in ministry. He praised the Philippians for their progress and exhorted them to keep growing in their strengths and weaknesses. Paul used Jesus' life as a model for believers. This short letter still encourages us even today.

Jesus showed us many examples of humility. One example is Jesus washing his disciple's feet. Another example is how Jesus told others that he came to serve not to be served.

Observation: An example of humility — One day a man was traveling with five colleagues. They were all from the same company. They went to stay in the house of a local person. There were three rooms in the house. The owner of the house and his wife took one room and there were two rooms left for the five people. When it was time to sleep, everyone went to the two rooms, but the boss remained behind. In the middle of the night one of the employees went to use the toilet and noticed the boss sleeping on the floor. It was clear that the boss wanted the employees to be comfortable and was ready to be uncomfortable for their sake.

▶ **Question**: Are you showing humility in your daily life? How?

▶ **Action Point**: Read and apply *Philippians 2:3-11*. This is the most famous passage in the entire Bible on the topic of humility.

Colossians

A man named Epaphras became a Christian through the ministry of Paul in Ephesus, and took the Gospel to a place called Colossae (*1:7-8; Acts 19:10*). The Colossians had fallen into false teaching that combined several human philosophies including Jewish laws, Greek religion and mystery cults. These false teachings said Jesus Christ did not have a physical body. They separated the spiritual realm from the physical realm because they believed what happened in the physical world could not affect the spiritual world. They denied that Jesus was truly human. In response to these wrong teachings, Paul emphasized that Christ is Supreme in everything and in every way, including salvation.

God the Father is invisible, but Christ shows us the Father exactly. If we want to see what God is like, we look to Jesus. Christ is Supreme over creation. He is not a created being. He took part in creation (*1:15-16*). Christ existed before creation (*1:17*). Christ is Supreme over all things, including the church (*1:18*).

> *Christ is the visible image of the invisible God. He existed before anything was created and is Supreme over all creation, for through Him God created everything in the Heavenly realms and on earth. He made the things we can see and the things we can't see, such as thrones, kingdoms, rulers, and authorities in the unseen world. Everything was created through Him and for Him.*

1 & 2 Thessalonians

Paul visited Thessalonica on his second missionary journey. *See Acts 16:9-17:5* to better understand the story.

Thessalonica was the capital city of Greece. Paul and his team went first to Philippi, then to Thessalonica. As a mob started a riot against them, the Christians sent Paul and Silas away. Paul sent Timothy back to Thessalonica. Timothy brought a report to Paul with questions from the church. Paul was in Corinth when he wrote the letter of 1 Thessalonians about many topics, including the Trinity, the deity of Christ, the Scriptures, the Second coming of Christ and the Resurrection. The letter gave the readers a firm foundation of doctrine. Paul wrote *2 Thessalonians* later that year or the next year; but still, false teaching spread in the church.

Observation: One of the leaders in TTI was preaching the Gospel in a small village. Some of the villagers were unhappy that people were coming to Christ so they placed a false claim against this leader with the local police. The man was sent to jail for 30 days. It was a discouragement to the ministry but after the man's release a TTI training center was established. Now 25 church planters are being trained there! It is easy to be discouraged when persecution comes. Our faith should grow when persecution comes (*2 Thes. 3:5*). Early believers counted it a privilege when persecution came.

▶ **Question**: How will you respond when you face persecution?

1 & 2 Timothy & Titus

The Pastoral Epistles are made up of three books in the New Testament: *First* and *Second Timothy*, and *Titus*. Churches are built around Jesus Christ and Paul's words in these three books. As a disciple who makes disciples, these three books will often be in your mind and heart. The Pastoral Epistles tells us how a new and existing church must function. The titles of the books come from the names of the men the letters were written to, Timothy and Titus. They were two of Paul's closest friends and church planters on his missionary team.

1 Timothy: This letter was written between 63-66 AD. Timothy needed to be instructed about how a church should be led. Paul wrote the letter to "defend sound doctrine and maintain sound discipline." The role of a church leader is to defend sound doctrine and promote solid discipline.

2 Timothy: This letter was written between 67-68 AD. This was the last book of the Bible Paul ever wrote before he was executed. Paul was in prison at the time he wrote this letter. Christians must remain faithful to sound doctrine when being persecuted.

Titus: This letter was written between 62 and 66 AD. Titus faced many problems in the church in Crete. Paul sent this letter to him to encourage him to be a good church leader. Sound doctrine leads to good works in Christ, after our conversion to Jesus.

Godly Leaders

Church leaders (elders and deacons) are called to be full of righteous character. The culture that surrounds the church might be the complete opposite of righteousness! This may include abuse of alcohol and sexual immorality. <u>This means that church leaders must be the same person inside and outside of the church</u>. They must not display godly qualities during gatherings or your main worship times and get drunk on the other days of the week. This means that there may be times when church leaders wisely avoid parts of their village that may cause them to fall.

Godly Leaders Understand the Proper use of Money (*Titus 1:7-11*)

1. The danger of greed: Greed is the desire for more. Greed will lead to other, immoral actions. Greed shows a lack of trust in God.

2. Contentment means being happy with what God has already provided.

3. Good overseers of money: Using it for your basic needs. Giving it away to those in need. God provides the wisdom for all decisions.

<u>Observation</u>: Many areas are too poor to offer money or valuable possessions to their church and leaders, but you can honor them by sharing food, livestock, or services for one another. Those who are wealthy may show God's love by providing for those who are less fortunate. This is in order to share the love of God and spread the Gospel. Many neighbors may not know Jesus. Sharing Christ's love through acts of service can be a way to give an opportunity for evangelism and church planting.

Other Religions

1. It is very likely that other religions will exist in the same area as your church.

   - Those who come to know Jesus must leave any beliefs in conflict with Jesus and the Scriptures. Christians cannot serve both their former religion and Christ. New believers must be patient and work hard at maintaining relationships when possible for the sake of love and compassion.

- Leaving your former lifestyle may very well result in persecution spiritually, physically, emotionally, or in another way. So it must be done by the wisdom of God.

2. There may be those who wish to keep their faith in Jesus a secret to avoid persecution. This may help to protect their families from becoming targets of violence by those who oppose the Truth. While we understand this behavior, these people are not good choices for church leadership. A church leader cannot keep his faith a secret forever.

- Church leaders can work to provide greater acceptance of Christianity so that people no longer feel forced to keep their faith a secret.

- Christians may need to open their households to those who are kicked out of their own house for becoming Christians.

Godly Leaders are Disciplined in Study and Prayer
(*2 Timothy 2:1-6, 2:15, 3:16-17, Titus 1:9*)

1. <u>A godly leader is committed to a lifetime of studying the Word of God</u>.

2. Prayer is a part of a leader's personal life. All benefit from setting aside regular time for prayer. God desires frequent prayers.

- Leaders pray for specific things, such as guidance, meeting other's needs, listening and responding to the Holy Spirit.

- Leaders also thank God. Prayers of thanksgiving help to fight against the temptation of greed. Prayers of thankfulness help a lifestyle of joy and gratitude.

Godly Leaders are First Servants: Jesus was and is a Servant. We follow His example:

- To be filled with the Spirit means to be controlled by the Spirit. Our intelligence, emotions and desire as well as physical powers all become available for achieving the purposes of God, when we are controlled by the Holy Spirit.

Godly Leaders Value Godly Relationships in the Church Family
(2 Timothy 4:9, 4:19-22, Titus 2:1-8)

- The church family will contain people from many different backgrounds.

- All members of the church family are worthy of honor.

- In some cases, there may be those inside the church who have hurt one another before they became Christians or even afterward. These people must be willing to sit down and deal honestly with the hurt, willing to move forward in forgiveness.

Godly Leaders Promote Healthy Homes *(Titus 2:1-8)*

- Not everyone in the house may be a Christian. This can be an opportunity, because it means that Christians have the wonderful opportunity to share Christ with their parents and children.

- Godly leaders love and value their spouse for their service in the home.

- Godly leaders remain faithful to their spouse.

  ▶ Not seeking sexual satisfaction with another person.

  ▶ Single Christians remain sexually pure.

Godly Leaders Respond to False Teachings
(2 Timothy 4:3-5, Titus 3:9-11)

Persecution

1. <u>The church will be persecuted</u>. Jesus promised that the world would hate Christians.

2. Christians must not resist persecution through violence. This may mean that Christians are forced to witness violence against their church and their family. We protect our families and have the right to protect them but we do not initiate violence. The best response may be to flee the situation with your family.

3. Christians may remember that Christ was persecuted for us. We find hope and joy in the fact that He is coming again.

Assignment

What do you understand about godly character? Write down your answers below:

▶ **Action Point**: What is one way you can serve the people in your community this week? Example: Wash a neighbor's cycle/bike, give food to the poor, help out people who are struggling.

Philemon

While Paul was under house arrest in Rome, one of the people he met was a slave named Onesimus. In these days slavery was very common. Onesimus was a slave in the household of a Christian named Philemon (a friend of Paul). Onesimus had run away from his owner and was trying to escape. In these days, a runaway slave could be captured and killed. But Paul encouraged Onesimus to return to his master and asked Philemon to forgive and treat him more like a brother than a slave.

▶ **Question**: In your life is there anything you are running away from? What sins are you hiding or not dealing with? Take time and evaluate what you must do to make all your relationships right.

▶ **Action Point**:

- What do you learn from Paul?

- What do you learn from Philemon?

- What do you learn from Onesimus?

Hebrews

Hebrews is a major book in the New Testament. The theme of *Hebrews* is that Jesus Christ holds the highest place in God's plan for salvation. Jesus is the Final Revelation. He is the last Word. He is the Final Sacrifice. Jesus Christ brings the "*new promise*." The new promise is better than the old promise.

Hebrews lists many examples of men and women who are known for their faith. Faith sees the things we hope for as real "*Faith is the confi-*

dence that what we hope for will actually happen; it gives us assurance about things we cannot see." (11:1).

Observation: One of the Old Testament hero's mentioned is Abraham. God promised to bless Abraham and his descendants. Abraham did not have any children to continue the family. Finally, in his old age, Abraham had a son named Isaac. God went to Abraham and told him to take his son (named Isaac) and sacrifice him on the top of a mountain. In the midst of all the questions he had, he trusted God. On the way, Isaac asked where the animal for the sacrifice was, as he did not know what was about to happen. Abraham answered that God would provide one. He took Isaac to the top of the mountain, made an altar, and tied Isaac to it. As Abraham was about to make the sacrifice, God stopped him and provided an animal in Isaac's place. God has also provided the Lamb of God, Jesus Christ, as the final solution 2000 years after Abraham (See *Genesis 22* for the whole story).

God tested Abraham when he told him to sacrifice his son. Abraham's strong faith in God made him the father of the faithful. Abraham had faith in God's plan (*11:17-19*; See *Gen. 22*).

Consider the stories of some others who showed great faith listed in the book of Hebrews:

- Isaac, Jacob and Joseph: They all believed God would keep His promise in the future (*11:20-22*; see Gen. *28:10-22; 48:1-20; 50:24-25*).

- Moses: God showed His plan for His people in the life of Moses and delivering the Israelites from Egypt. Moses responded with faith (*11:23-29*; see *Ex. 2:1-3, 11-15; 10:28; 12:21; 14:22-29*).

- Joshua and Jericho: God promised His people a new land. Joshua led the people by faith (*11:30*; see *Josh. 6:20*).

- Rahab: She was not an Israelite, but God saved her from destruction because of her faith (*11:31*; see *Josh. 6:23*).

- Many more were people of faith: Gideon (see *Judg. 6:11*), Barak (*Judg. 4:6-24*), Samson (*Judg. 13:24*), Jephthah (*Judg. 11:1-29*), David (*1 Sam. 16:17-18*), Samuel (*1 Sam. 7:9-14*).

James

The writer is the half-brother of Jesus (*Mat. 13:55*). James became the leader of the Church in Jerusalem (*Act. 15:13, Gal. 2:9*). The readers were Christians who lived outside of Palestine. James has a practical purpose. The theme is: "If you believe in Jesus, your actions will show it."

▶ **Question**: Look up *James 1:27* and answer the following question: What is true religion?

True religion is not based on ceremonies or rituals. It is doing what God wanted us to do in the world, without taking on the wrong values of the world.

▶ **Action Point**: What is your response to the orphans and widows in your community? What must you do?

1 & 2 Peter

Peter, one of the first twelve disciples of Jesus, wrote *1 and 2 Peter*. Tradition tells us that Peter died in Rome during a period of persecution, dying upside down on a cross. Peter wrote his first letter to encourage readers who suffered because of their Christian faith.

Second Peter talks about false teaching. His purpose was to speak against the false teachers so that his readers would not accept wrong teaching as truth. Peter warns readers about the coming judgment and urges them to remain faithful while they wait for Christ to return.

▶ **Question**: How do you prepare yourself to recognize and avoid false teachings? Hint: One area to focus on is what people say about Jesus. Rebuke or avoid anyone who teaches something different than the Gospel of Christ, or contrary to Scripture.

The Letters of John

The author of the *Gospel of John* also wrote the letters of *John*. John died at the end of the first century. Many lies and false teachings were spreading and coming into the church.

1 John

John wrote the first letter to help his readers know how to decide if a teaching was false. John used the word love 46 times in five chapters. John commanded us to test the motivation behind every teaching (*1 John 4:1*). John stressed the connection between true faith and love in action.

Reminder: You will certainly come across false teachers. It is to your benefit to remember and put into practice the lessons taught using the SWORD method as you study Scripture! This will help you to avoid false teaching!

2 John

Always watch out for false teaching that changes or manipulates the truth about who Jesus is. Walk in Truth and Love, and then be careful about "deceivers". Anyone who does not teach that Jesus is God in human flesh is not teaching truth (See *1 John 4:2-3*). There is unusual joy when we as believers are able to walk consistently with the Lord and be together in fellowship.

3 John

John writes to show approval to Gaius, who supported the messengers John sent. Gaius remained faithful. As a result this brought joy to John. There is no greater joy than to know that physical children and spiritual children you raised are walking with the Lord. When we support the ministry of other people, we share in their work (*7-8*).

> ▶ **Question**: Jesus said "they will know you are My disciples by your love.' How are you showing love to others? Are you known for your love?

> ▶ **Action Point**: Think of one person you can go and show the love of Christ today!

Jude

In *Matthew 13:55*, there is a record of Jesus' half-brothers. Jude, the author of this letter, is one of them. False teachers said that being saved by grace meant it did not matter if Christians sinned. Jude wrote to warn readers about this dangerous doctrine. This philosophy teaches that the soul is trapped in the body. Only the soul is spiritual. Humans may do anything they want with the body because it is not spiritual. Christians have true knowledge and do not have to worry about sins in the body. As apostles, Paul and Peter wrote to correct this false teaching, Jude also wrote with this purpose.

False teachers rejected authority because they had lost their connection to the Truth. They did not submit to people in authority in the church. The false teachers faced judgment (*14-16*).

Pay attention to the apostles teaching as the Lord Jesus Himself gave them authority. Watch out for false teachers. Jude says they do not even have the Spirit. Without the Spirit, they are not saved (See *Rom 8:9*). Grow in God's grace and care for others (*20-23*).

Now all glory to God, who is able to keep you from falling away and will bring you with great joy into his glorious presence without a single fault. All glory to him who alone is God, our Savior through Jesus Christ our Lord. All glory, majesty, power, and authority are his before all time, and in the present, and beyond all time! Amen. (*24-25*).

Revelation

The writer of *Revelation* is John who wrote the *Gospel of John* and letters of *1-3 John*. Under the rule of Emperor Domitian, Christians suffered persecution because they would not worship the Roman emperor. As punishment for the Christian's activities, John was a prisoner on the island of Patmos (*1:9*). The book of *Revelation* records the visions and messages John received while he was there. The book of *Revelation* is full of symbolic language.

John wrote to encourage Christians to stand firm against emperor worship. The theme of *Revelation* is God's control of history. Human history will come to an end. At that time, the wicked will be destroyed.

The book of Revelation was given to believers so that they can be sure that Christ will return one day and God's people will enter eternal glory. We can be confident of the promise of Jesus who said He would return one day. The Bible very clearly explains that He will come back for His church and establish His Kingdom on earth. All who came to Jesus Christ in faith will be in eternity with Him. Those who believe and live godly lives will reign and rule with Him and those who reject Jesus will be in eternal separation. As a child of God we should be prepared and ready, as well as prepare others for His return.

Learning the New Testament is wonderful for our life and ministry in Jesus Christ.

> ▶ **Action Point**: Read at least one chapter from the New Testament each day. Use the New Testament Reading Guide at the end of this book to keep on track.

We are Not Just "Hearers" of the Word, but "Doers" (James 1:22)

We are doers of God's Word, not just hearers.

Like a man that built his house upon a rock:

The rains came...

The house stood firm.

Whoever hears and does not do what God says

Is like a man that built his house upon the sand:

The rains came...

The house fell.

Which man are you like?

How will you apply what you have learned this week?

Chapter 7
Important Bible Doctrines

Imagine someone in your village or city asks you what you believe. You begin to tell them about Jesus and His love for them. You quote Bible verses to them. You answer their questions. What are you doing? You are doing *theology* or *teaching doctrine*.

Theology is the study of God. It is the Christian discipline that studies God, His character and His works that are revealed in the Bible. The goal is to apply God's Truth to life, to live for God more consistently, love Him more deeply, and serve Him fully.

Nothing could be more exciting than to study about our wonderful God, who has saved us and called us into His ministry. We are on a mission with Him to seek and save the lost!

What is doctrine?

- The word *doctrine* means *sound teaching*. For our purpose, it is helpful to define doctrine as *what the Bible teaches about a topic*. For example, what does the Bible teach about sin, creation, or death?

- A house built with blocks can illustrate the relationship between doctrine and theology. Doctrines are the building blocks used to build the house, and theology is the house itself, for it is a more complete picture of God, His purposes and what He is doing.

Basics of Christian Theology

The basics of Christian theology are that God exists and that *He has spoken to us*. It is important to note that we begin this study with the belief that God exists, and we can know Him because He has spoken to us through His Word, the Bible.

Why Should You Study Doctrine?

- The better you know God, the more passionate your worship of Him will be.

- To be more effective in sharing the Gospel with people in your community.

- Everyone has a view of the world: what the meaning of life is, what the problem with the world is, and what the possible solution may be.

- By understanding doctrine, we get a clear understanding of how God's Word answers these basic questions, so we can show God's Truth to people who do not know Him.

- Studying doctrine will make your beliefs stronger about God's mission and your involvement in it.

<u>You should approach this study with a grateful heart and a strong dependence on the leadership of the Holy Spirit.</u>

How Will Knowing Theology Help Me as a Disciple who Makes Disciples and a Church Planter?

- I will know God better. Because good theology describes God and His character accurately, I can know Him more intimately as a result of studying theology. I will know more about the Father, Jesus, and the Holy Spirit; and therefore love Him more, praise Him better, and serve Him fully.

- I will know the Truth of God better. Knowing the doctrines of salvation, the Scriptures, sin, future things, and other areas will give me a solid foundation in my study of the Bible.

- I will increasingly know the mission of God. Since God is a missional God, I will be able to be on mission with Him because I know His heart better.

- I will fulfill Paul's command to study to show myself approved unto God, a workman who does not need to be ashamed, rightly dividing the Word of Truth (2 Tim. 2:15).

- I will have more confidence in my story.

- I will be able to preach and teach with greater accuracy.

- I will be able to answer people's questions better.

- I will be able to defend the faith better.

Studying theology and the main doctrines in the Bible can change your life. It will cause you to know God better, trust Him more fully, and proclaim Him more boldly to others in your village or location. It will also provide a solid foundation and give you confidence as you plant and see Him grow a church for His glory.

Our Prayer Together

Now may the God of peace who brought up our Lord Jesus from the dead, that great Shepherd of the sheep, through the blood of the everlasting covenant, make you complete in every good work to do His will, working in you what is well pleasing in His sight, through Jesus Christ, to whom be glory forever and ever. Amen. (Hebrews 13:20-21)

The following pages include a basic statement of what we believe. Some call this a doctrinal statement or doctrinal position. We simply call it TTI's statement of faith, as it outlines the basics of what we believe. As you study the Scriptures more and more you will come to form a statement of faith for yourself as an individual as well as the church you plant. It is important to know what you believe and why you believe it!

TTI Statement of Faith

What We Believe

- In essential beliefs — we have Unity

  ▸ *"There is one Body and one Spirit... one Lord, one faith, one baptism, and one God and Father of us all..." Eph. 4:4-6*

- In non-essential beliefs — we have Liberty

  ▸ *"Receive one who is weak in the faith, but not to disputes over doubtful things...Who are you to judge another's servant? To his own master he stands or falls... So then each of us shall give an account of himself to God... Do you have faith? Have it to yourself before God." Rom. 14:1, 4, 12, 22*

- In all our beliefs — we show Charity

  ▸ *"And though I have the gift of prophecy, and understand all mysteries and all knowledge, and though I have all faith, so that I could remove mountains, but have not love, I am nothing." 1 Cor. 13:2*

The Essentials We Hold To:

- THE GODHEAD (TRINITY)
  - ▶ There is one God, eternally existent in three persons: Father, Son, and Holy Spirit. *Deut. 6:4*

- THE FATHER
  - ▶ The first person of the Godhead orders and directs all things according to His own purpose and pleasure. He authored, created, and sustains all things in the universe without any means other than His own pure power. By His grace, He involves Himself in the affairs of men, hears and answers prayer, and saves from sin and death all that come to Him through Jesus Christ. *Mat. 6:9, Eph. 1:3, Joh. 5:19*

- THE LORD JESUS CHRIST
  - ▶ He existed eternally as the second person of the Godhead. By His virgin birth He came to earth as fully God and fully man, living a sinless life. His death on the cross made atonement for man's sin, evidenced by His bodily resurrection from the dead. He physically ascended to the right hand of God the Father, and He will return in power and glory. *Joh. 1:14, Col. 2:9, Act. 2:33*

- THE HOLY SPIRIT
  - ▶ The third person of the Godhead convicts men of sin, regenerates, baptizes, indwells, instructs, and sets apart believers unto a holy life. We encourage all believers to seek a life of obedience to the leadership of the Holy Spirit. We believe this step is essential for empowering believers for victorious living and ministry through the gifts given by the Holy Spirit. *Titus 3:5, Act. 1:8, 1 Cor. 3:16*

- THE BIBLE
  - ▶ The Scriptures of the Old and New Testaments are the complete, inerrant in the original manuscripts, divinely inspired, infallible Word of God. The Bible is the supreme authority and guide for our Christian faith and living. *2 Pet. 1:20, Heb. 4:12*

- THE NATURE OF MANKIND
  - ▶ Mankind was directly created in God's image, voluntarily fell into sin by personal disobedience to the will of God; conse-

quently, all people are spiritually dead apart from Jesus Christ. The fall of humanity was a once-for-all historical fact. Its effect spread to all men, each of whom is born with a sinful nature and is in need of salvation. *Eph. 2:1, Rom. 3:10, Rom. 3:23-24*

- THE NECESSITY OF SALVATION
  - ▶ Salvation (Justification) is by grace, a gift of God apart from works. Salvation (Justification) includes repentance, a turning from one's own way to God's way. All who receive Jesus Christ are born-again, regenerated by the Holy Spirit, and become the children of God. Our relationship with Christ is secure not by our actions but by the sustaining power and love of God. A changed life follows the work of God in a person's Salvation (Justification). *Titus 2:11, 1 Joh. 1:9, 1 Pet. 2:2*

- THE CHURCH
  - ▶ The church is the body of believers consisting of all born-again persons without respect to race, culture, age or background. Directed by Jesus Christ and empowered by the Holy Spirit, the church is taking the good news of salvation to the whole world.
  - ▶ Our fellowship is inclusive rather than exclusive and stresses love for God and one another, the unity of all believers, and obedience to the Holy Spirit. *Eph. 2:19-21, Eph. 3:10*

- ABOUT ETERNITY
  - ▶ People were created to exist forever. We will either exist eternally separated from God by sin, or eternally with God through forgiveness and salvation. To be eternally separated from God is Hell. To be eternally in union with Him is eternal life. Heaven and Hell are real places of eternal existence. *Joh. 3:16; 14:17; Rom. 6:23; 8:17-18; Rev.20:15; 1 Cor. 2:7-9*

<u>Remember</u>: The goal of studying doctrine is to apply God's Truth to life, to live for God more consistently, love Him more deeply, and serve Him fully.

▶ **Question**: How will you do this?

▶ **Action Point**: Consider and memorize this simple and clear statement of faith known as the *Apostles Creed*. (Use the pictures on the following page to help you remember.)

I believe in God the Father, Almighty.

Creator of Heaven and earth.

I believe in Jesus Christ, His only Son, our Lord.

*I believe He was conceived by the Holy Spirit
and born of the Virgin Mary.*

*I believe He suffered under Pontius Pilate;
was crucified, died and was buried.*

I believe on the third day He rose again from the dead.

*I believe He ascended into Heaven, and is seated
at the right hand of God the Father Almighty.*

I believe from there He will come to judge the living and the dead.

I believe in the Holy Spirit:

I believe in the Universal church and the communion of saints.

I believe in the forgiveness of sins.

I believe in the resurrection of the body.

I believe in the life everlasting. Amen.

Major Bible Doctrines Summarized in Picture Form

I believe in God, the Father Almighty

Creator of heaven and earth

I believe in Jesus Christ, His only Son, our Lord

Who was conceived by the Holy Spirit

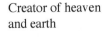

Born of the Virgin Mary

Suffered under Pontius Pilate

Was crucified, died

And was buried

On the third day He rose again from the dead

He ascended into heaven

And is seated at the right hand of God the Father Almighty

From there He will come to judge the living and the dead

I believe in the Holy Spirit

The Universal Church

The Communion of the Saints

The forgiveness of sins

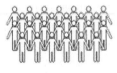

The resurrection of the body

And the life everlasting - Amen

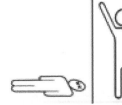

Chapter 8
How to Defend Your Faith

We begin this chapter by reminding you of the importance to not only know what you believe, but also the need to live what you believe daily in your walk with Jesus Christ. Our knowledge of God should be applied in our lifestyle.

"Instead, you must worship Christ as Lord of your life. And if someone asks about your Christian hope, always be ready to explain it" (*1 Peter 3:15*).

Every church planter must be ready to give an honest and truthful answer for what they believe and why they believe in God.

Defending Your Faith from Evidence in History

1. <u>We can trust the Bible</u>. The Bible is trustworthy and was written by eyewitnesses who told the truth.

2. <u>In the Bible, Jesus claimed to be God</u>. His followers understood the claims He made and so did His enemies. They said: *"You, being a man, make yourself out to be God"* (*John 10:30-33*).

3. <u>Jesus proved His claim to be God by rising from the dead three days after He was crucified</u>. He was also seen by over 500 people who confirmed this fact.

The Historical Evidence for the Bible

The Gospels were written during Jesus' generation.

1. The writers could not make up false stories, as the other eyewitnesses would have rejected their claims if they were not true (*2 Pet. 1:16*).

2. Luke and the other Gospel writers wrote with the purpose of recording actual history. (*Luke 1:1-4*).

3. The Gospels are extremely consistent with each other.

4. Many of the authors were martyred for their faith in Jesus.

5. Studies of ancient cities have proven the accuracy of Scripture when it describes the places, locations and customs of first century culture.

6. There was plenty of opportunity for eyewitnesses to disagree with the Gospel accounts, but no one argues that Jesus performed great signs and wonders and that He had a large group of followers.

In the Bible, Jesus Claims to be God

John 10:30-33: Jesus claims to be of one nature with God the Father. This caused the Jews to want to stone Him for claiming He was God.

Mark 2:5: By claiming that He could forgive sins. He claimed that He was God and this offended the Jews who were there.

Mark 14:61-64: Jesus clearly admits that He is the Son of God. He used the Hebrew word *Yahweh*, translated *I am*. *Yahweh* was the personal name for God found in *Exodus 6*. This name was so precious to Jews that they would never even speak the word. But Jesus said it – and He said it about Himself. He is *Yahweh*.

Jesus Rose from the Dead

The resurrection of Jesus Christ is the most important event in history. The Apostle Paul admits, "A*nd if Christ has not been raised, then your faith is useless ... we are more to be pitied than anyone in the world"* (*1 Cor. 15:17,19*). Jesus did rise from the dead, so we have hope for the future, confidence in God's promises and victory over sin (*1 Cor. 15:50-58*).

1. There was no way anyone could have survived the brutal torture that Jesus was put through by the Roman soldiers (*Luke. 22:44*).

2. His body was taken down off the cross and given to Joseph, a friend who was a member of the ruling council. He was a public figure so it would be no secret where he buried Jesus (*Luke 23:50-51*). A huge stone covered the tomb where Jesus was buried. It was so heavy that twenty men could not roll it away. There were trained guards guarding the tomb (*Mt. 27:65-66*).

3. Jesus was in the tomb for three days and then rose again. The Jews who did not believe never argued that the tomb was empty, they only asked, "What happened to the body?"

4. <u>The disciples knew that Jesus had been resurrected, and all but one of them was martyred for their faith and belief in Jesus and His resurrection</u>.

5. Jesus appeared to John, to the twelve disciples, and at one time to 500 people (*1 Cor. 15:3-8*).

<u>Observation</u>: God has revealed Himself: In creation, in man's conscience, in the life of Christ and in the Scriptures (*Psa. 19:1-6, Rom. 1:18-20, John.1:1-4, 14*). All truth is from God and complete. God does not change, therefore truth does not change.

Understanding Worldviews and Cultures

A worldview is the way you look at the world. Every person and every culture has their own worldview. We must understand the local cultural beliefs that make people believe what they believe and live the way they live if we are going to effectively share Christ (*1 Pet. 3:15-16*). When you are among people of similar culture this is easy. However, when you cross cultures or worldviews it is important to understand the perspective of the person you are working with.

Monotheism (Belief in One God): Christianity, Islam and Judaism are all monotheistic religions. This is the belief that there is one powerful and personal being who is beyond this physical world. This being also created the universe and everything in it for His glory.

Atheism: Atheism believes that no God exists. And because God does not exist, humans evolved randomly from lesser things and have no real purpose. Life ends with death and evil is human ignorance.

Pantheism: Pantheists believe that there is no creator beyond the universe and that the universe is not real. Rather, the universe is a picture of god (called Brahman), who is the real life force in the universe. The religions that are pantheistic are mainly Hinduism, and Zen Buddhism.

Panentheism: Panentheism is the belief that god is in the world the way a soul or mind is in a body; god is in a continual process of change. Parts of panentheism can be found in Hinduism, Islam, Judaism, Kabbalism, and Gnosticism.

Deism: Deism is the idea that God set the universe and world in motion and then let things go on their own. He exists but is not personal and humanity is the result of natural processes of the universe. Man only needs to be moral and rational. Evil comes from ignorance.

Polytheism: Polytheism is the idea that there are many gods. These gods often have long histories and interact with other gods and goddesses. These gods also typically have similar traits to humans but with some extra powers, abilities, or knowledge. This is found mainly in Hinduism.

Finite godism: This philosophy teaches that God exists but He is limited in His power. God is not infinite in His power, wisdom or control. He is limited in what He can do and evil simply exists because God is not powerful enough to overcome.

Animism: This belief teaches there are spiritual forces that can be manipulated according to a person's desires through rituals and charms. Animism teaches people to fill voids in their life with personal spirit-beings and to achieve divine oneness with their gods. Animists believe in both personal spirit-beings and in impersonal spiritual forces. They believe spirit-beings can embody deceased ancestors, while other spirit-beings are not embodied. They believe spirit-beings can exert influence over nature (i.e. storms, thunder, fields, seas, etc.) and over human activities (i.e. marriage, businesses, war, death, birth, etc.). They attribute spiritual power to any object, and believe that they can utilize the spiritual energy in these objects according to their own will.

Action Point: Take some time to evaluate these worldviews and identify those that you relate with and understand best. Also, consider those in your village and surrounding area. How do they view things? Consider this as you talk with them.

World Religions and Cults

What is a religion? A religion is a belief between man and a being believed to be God, which usually results in a commitment of faith, acts of service and a lifestyle of obedience.

What is a cult? A cult is a religious group dedicated to a leader or teachings that are in contradiction or outright denial of basic Biblical truths.

Discuss this quote: **"If you can argue someone into believing in Christ, then someone else can probably argue them out of believing in Christ."**

All of our efforts must focus on sharing who Jesus is, what He has done, and why His Truth claims are valid. There are thousands of false ideas and philosophies that compete for our attention. It is the Christian's job to contest for truth and dismiss false teaching, because many are looking for answers. Some are desperately hungry for the truth and it is the job of the Christian to make sure they receive it.

We should never give up on people that are resistant or opposed to the Christian faith, but we must keep in mind that we cannot argue people into belief. We can provide evidence and give reasons for what we believe. We can also reflect the love of God to everyone. *"He who has ears to hear let him hear!"* (*Mat. 11:15*).

The following pages give a basic introduction and summary of different world religions and cults.

ISLAM

Islam means submission to Allah. Started by Muhammad, following what he claimed to be revelations from the angel Gabriel and recorded in 114 chapters of the Quran, Islam is built on five essential pillars:

1. <u>Shahadah</u>: "I bear witness that there is no God but Allah and that Mohammed is his messenger."
2. <u>Salat</u>: Praying 5 times every day.
3. <u>Sawm</u>: Fasting during Ramadan (Ramazan).
4. <u>Zakat</u>: Giving 2.5% of income to the poor.
5. <u>Hajj</u>: Journey to the holy city of Mecca at least once in a lifetime.

Muslim theology:

1. **God (Allah) is one**.

2. **Jesus Christ** — He was one of the Major Prophets born of a virgin, but not the Son of God. They deny Jesus died on the cross. They also believe Jesus was sinless.

3. **Sin and Salvation** — Salvation is based on good works, and only Allah can allow anyone into Heaven. Sin can be forgiven through repentance, yet there are no guarantees you will be allowed into Heaven. It all depends on the mercy of Allah.

4. **Holy Books** — Islam views the Bible as corrupted and the *Qur'an* is the Word of Allah.

When witnessing, do not be critical of Mohammed, Allah, or the *Qur'an*. Focus on the love of God with prayer and faith. Understand that only through the work of Jesus on the cross and the conviction of the Holy Spirit can one come to salvation. Forgiveness of sins comes by grace through faith.

HINDUISM

Hinduism has no one central creed or doctrinal statement. However, there are a few core beliefs that many profess:

1. **God** — Beyond the principal gods of the *Trimurti* (three manifestations including *Brahma*, *Vishnu*, and *Shiva*), there are 330,000,000 gods.

2. **Jesus Christ** — Jesus is one of many gods.

3. **Sin and Salvation** — Sin is as a result of ignorance. Salvation is earned through good works (fasting, rituals, etc.), which brings good karma. The ultimate goal of a Hindu is to be free from the cycle of karma and from life's suffering when they finally are absorbed back into the ultimate reality (Brahman).

4. **Karma** is the idea that an action leads to consequences. If a person can build up good karma in this life then he will be born into a higher life in the next life; but if he builds up bad karma in this life then he will be born into a lower life in the next life. Karma does not allow forgiveness. This continual cycle of death and rebirth is called (sansara) reincarnation.

5. **Holy Books** — Hinduism uses a collection of prayers and hymns called the *Vedas*. The last of the *Vedas*, called the *Upanishads*, include the concept that there is one ultimate reality called *Brahman* behind many gods. Hindus also use the *Bhagavad-Gita* which is a less authoritative but more popular scripture written around 500 BC.

When witnessing to the Hindu, help him or her see that God is personal and we can relate to Him without fear. God is loving, caring, and He loves all human beings regardless of their sin.

THE PROSPERITY GOSPEL

This is the teaching that God wants believers to be materially wealthy and healthy. All we need is to have faith in prayers and we will have all our wants supplied. You see it, like, claim it by faith and it is yours.

1. Giving or the "*law of compensation*" is central to this doctrine. You give so you can receive back! Faith is in one's desire rather than the Bible and if one does not get their desires, it is because they do not have enough faith.
2. Prosperity Gospel suggests that poverty is a sin.
3. **God** is limited to a deity who is only there to meet our selfish, individual needs.

In witnessing, help them understand that the **central** message of the Bible is a Person, Who is God, Jesus Christ. His life and those of His disciples were never focused on prosperity but on faithful obedience to God and sacrificial living. The focus must always be on Jesus Christ. Jesus is not a path to the goal; rather He is the goal itself. He is the Way, The Truth and The Life. Jesus is the Message.

HARE KRISHNA

Krishna is a Hindu avatar through which Hinduism's preeminent god, Vishnu, protects the universe. Krishna is more revered than Vishnu. They share many beliefs with Hinduism.

1. **God** — Krishna is the essence of all existence, the "Supreme Personality of God."

2. **Jesus Christ** — He is below Krishna and some believe He is Krishna's son.

3. **Sin and Salvation** — Sin is ignorance and salvation is from reincarnation. One must enter into a personal relationship with Krishna by submitting to a spiritual master and chanting a mantra, which removes one's focus from material desires and places it on Krishna. Once a person attains Krishna consciousness, he or she will no longer be subject to reincarnation.

In witnessing to them, help them see that there would be an obvious improvement in human nature after thousands of years of reincarnations. However reality shows a different picture with spiritual, economic and social problems everywhere.

BUDDHISM

Started by Budha, Siddhartha Gautama lived in a palace where he was sheltered from suffering. He wandered away from the palace one day and encountered suffering. This made him unsatisfied with wealth and he tried to find a solution to suffering. He would come up with the Four Noble Truths that form a pillar of Buddhism.

1. Life consists of suffering, which includes pain, misery, and sorrow.

2. Suffering comes from desiring those things that are impermanent. Everything is changing and impermanent.

3. Eliminating desire of those things that are impermanent is the way to free oneself from suffering.

4. Desire is removed by following the Eightfold Path: Right understanding. Right thinking. Right speech. Right action. Right livelihood. Right effort. Right awareness. Right meditation.

5. **God** is abstract and unknowable.

6. **Jesus Christ** is a spiritual master possibly equal to Buddha.

7. **Sin and Salvation** — Suffering is the result of desire that is temporary. Salvation comes when we stop all desire and empty the mind to enter the *Nirvana*, where self is extinguished and ultimate enlightenment is attained.

8. **Scripture** — *Tripitaka* the "three baskets" of teachings include Buddha's teachings, rules for monks and philosophical teachings. Others include the *Lotus Sutra* and *Perfection of Wisdom* writings along with the *Tripitaka* as Scripture.

In witnessing, begin with what we have in common, such as the danger of excess desire that leads to suffering, the value of prayer, compassion and self-discipline. However point out the difference between Buddha and Jesus. Only Jesus can deliver us from the excess desires of life and the suffering that results. Jesus does away with karma debt by paying for our sins with His death on the cross.

ANIMISM / SANTERIA

Animism is the belief that all objects and events in the universe have spiritual force and significance. Santeria is a religion that comes from the Animism worldview.

1. **God** is a distant, impersonal and unknowable force and can be manipulated through rituals and charms.

2. Animists believe in both personal spirit-beings and in impersonal spiritual forces. They believe spirit-beings can embody dead ancestors, while other spirit-beings are not embodied. These spirit-beings can have influence over nature (i.e. storms, thunder, fields, seas, etc.) and over human activities (i.e. marriage, death, birth, businesses, war, etc.).

3. **Sin and Salvation** — Sin is offending the ancestors and/or the spirit beings. People will know they have sinned when bad things happen to them and to earn salvation, people will sacrifice to these spirit beings in order to appease them.

4. They use diviners to contact and communicate with the spirit beings. Some animists believe that a person's spirit continues to exist after death through reincarnation in another human body, while others think a deceased person becomes an ancestral spirit who has power to bless or curse the family and so the family must give offerings to appease him or her.

In witnessing to an Animist focus on sacrifice and how Jesus has made His own once and for all, offering us eternal salvation and hope.

JUDAISM

Some follow strict traditions and the rabbinic interpretations of the laws of Moses. Others focus on the OT prophets and ethics over the traditions of the Rabbis. Judaism holds strongly to the Sh'ma which proclaims *"Listen, O Israel! The Lord is our God, the Lord alone"* (*Deut. 6:4*).

1. **God** is personal, eternal, all-powerful, all knowing, and all-present.

2. **Jesus** is not the Messiah. The Messiah is a political figure who will restore the Jewish kingdom and bring justice. Others believe that the Messiah is not a person but a period of time ("Messianic Age") when humanity will reach its ultimate perfection.

3. **Sin** is breaking the commandments and repentance comes through obedience to the Law. They believe in the Old Testament, The Hebrew Scriptures

In witnessing to those who follow Judaism, simply concentrate on Jesus Christ and His Grace. Read to them *Isaiah 52* and *53*. Have them read the end of all four Gospels regarding the Final Week/Passion Week of Jesus Christ. Ask them, how can Jesus not be the Messiah of *Isaiah 52* and *53*?

ROMAN CATHOLICISM

Roman Catholics believe that Peter was set apart by Christ and afterwards traveled to Rome where he founded a church and served as its first bishop, becoming the first pope.

1. Roman Catholics believe that **God** is Trinity: Father, Son and Holy Spirit.

2. **Jesus** is the Son of God, born of virgin Mary, lived a sinless life, died on the cross for sins and rose from the grave, ascended to Heaven and will come again.

3. Good works accompanied by faith, grace and baptism (which they view as a requirement) are the way of salvation.

4. Baptism is a cleansing ceremony and sprinkling with water is acceptable. They promote the baptizing of infants.

5. Priests have a central mediation role. Individuals confess their sins to the priests, who represent Christ, and receive cleansing.

6. They pray to Mary and saints to intercede for them to God. They possess and look to relics/statues of saints for miracles and cures, and they say prayers to a rosary.

7. Their Mass centers on the Eucharist (Communion/ Lords Supper); they believe the bread literally turns into the body of Jesus and the wine His blood when the priests place their hands over them.

8. **Scripture**: the church is equal with Scripture. The Pope's words are faultless and binding on them when he speaks *ex cathedra* (from the chair).

In witnessing to them, encourage them to examine their beliefs in light of what the Bible says about grace. Move them away from works salvation and to grace through faith salvation. Use *Ephesians* to help them grasp grace.

JEHOVAH'S WITNESSES

Founded by Charles Russell in 1879.

1. **God** — Jehovah is the one true God and must be addressed with the personal name Jehovah. They deny the Trinity.

2. **Jesus Christ** — Jesus and the archangel Michael are the same. He died on a stake (not a cross) and was raised as a spirit being. He returned spiritually in 1914 and has been ruling invisibly on earth through the Watchtower Society.

3. **Sin and Salvation** — Salvation is not possible apart from obedience to the Watchtower and being faithful to distributing Watchtower tracts door-to-door. Christ's death removed the inherited sin from Adam and the individual must work his way toward salvation.

4. **Scripture** — Jehovah's Witnesses hold to the *Watchtower Society* and the *New World Translation* as their authority, which is an incorrect translation of the Bible.

In talking with a Jehovah's Witness make sure you are comparing your beliefs by using the Holy Bible, not their Bible. Try to focus on the saving grace of Christ, His work on the cross and the free gift of salvation apart from works.

MORMONISM

Started by Joseph Smith, he claimed to have received six visions from an angel Moroni who told him of a book written on gold plates, which gave an account of the former inhabitants of America and also the true gospel.

1. **God** — was a man who became God by living a perfect life. Men can become gods by holding to Mormonism. Mormons believe that the Trinity is three separate gods.

2. **Jesus Christ** — "the elder brother," was the spirit child of the Father. He was the Jehovah of the Old Testament before his incarnation and became a man through a sexual relationship between the father (who was flesh and one) and Mary.

3. Jesus and Satan are spirit brothers and sons of God.

4. **Sin and Salvation** — Salvation is <u>by good works</u> and forgiveness of sins comes by faith, repentance and baptism by an approved Mormon priest.

5. **Scripture** — the *Book of Mormon, Doctrine and Covenants,* and the *Pearl of Great Price.*

In witnessing simply help them understand that humans cannot become gods nor attain perfection through their good works.

ONENESS THEOLOGY

Baptizing in the name of Jesus, they believe that the Father, Son and Holy Spirit are all expressions of Jesus. Salvation includes faith, repentance, and water baptism in the name of Jesus only and that one's baptism in the Holy Spirit will be signified by speaking in tongues.

1. **God** — Jesus is the Father, Son and Holy Spirit revealed in three different modes/roles that Jesus temporarily adopts.

2. **Sin and Salvation** — Salvation is maintained by holiness not by God's grace

3. **Scripture** — The Bible is God's revelation to man even though they misinterpret it.

In witnessing focus on the interaction between the Trinity, especially in the creation story and the baptism of Jesus. Emphasize that Jesus is not the summation of the Trinity, but the physical expression of the Father while He lived here on earth (*John. 1*). He is the second Person of the Trinity.

BAHA'I

Mizra Ali Muhammad (the "Bab," meaning the Gate) claiming to be a direct descendent of the prophet Mohammed considered himself the second coming of Christ.

1. God — God is the "Supreme Singleness," and is unknowable. Truth is found in all religions.
2. Jesus Christ — Jesus is just one of many prophets.
3. Sin and Salvation — sin is something people learn and can be unlearned. <u>Salvation is earned by personal works</u>.
4. Scripture — God has progressively revealed himself through diverse manifestations such as Adam, Noah, Abraham, Moses, Jesus, Mohammed, Zoroaster, Buddha, and Abdul Baha. But the original Baha'u'llah's writings, Kitab-i-Aqdas (the Book of Certitude) is considered the sacred Scripture by Baha'is.

While witnessing to Baha'is be sure to have them read *John 1-3* and focus on the uniqueness of Jesus Christ.

SIKHISM

Sikhism originally tried to resolve conflict between Islam and Hinduism.

1. **God** — they believe in one God who cannot be seen, but also in karma and reincarnation.
2. **Jesus Christ** — Christ is a spiritual guide like Buddha.
3. **Sin and Salvation** — To eventually experience oneness with God's light by coming into harmony with the universe's order, one only needs to repeat a holy word or name as they meditate.

Discuss *John 14:1-6* with Sikhs, unfold the truths of this great text to them and dialogue with them on what this means.

THE NEW AGE MOVEMENT (YOGA)

1. **God** — Everything and everyone is god.

2. **Jesus Christ** — Jesus is a spiritual model and guru and is now a spiritual guide.

3. **Sin and Salvation** — overcome bad karma with good karma by using supernatural power through meditation, self-awareness and spirit guides.

Interact with these people on *Titus 2:11-15* and that Jesus is not just the Savior, but He is also God. Help them to see His superiority and man's inferiority.

CHRISTIAN SCIENCE

1. **God** — God is an impersonal force of life, truth, love, intelligence and spirit. God is all that truly exists. Matter is an illusion.

2. **Jesus Christ** — Jesus is a man who displayed the light of truth. "Christ" means perfection, not a person.

3. **Sin and Salvation** — Humanity is already eternally saved. Sin, evil, sickness and death are not real. Heaven and hell are states of mind. The way to reach Heaven is by attaining harmony (oneness with god).

Let the Word of God speak to the Christian Scientist through your prayers and care for them. Show them Jesus and His life here on earth in the Gospels and now through His Spirit, the Holy Spirit through you.

When talking to people from other religions and sects it is important to first remember that Jesus said they will know you are my disciples by your love.

We should care for the person first, love and pray for them. **We are not looking to win an argument or force someone to believe like we do.** It is not our job to convince them to believe in Christ, but simply ask the Holy Spirit to do His convicting work. Our job is to tell them about the Love of Christ, what He has done for us, and what He can do for them.

▸ **Action Point:** Consider at least one person of another religion/ sect. Begin praying that God will reveal Himself to them and be faithful to share the love of Christ with them.

Story to Share When Defending Your Faith

In the beginning there was God.

He created the heavens and the earth.

He created people to have friendship with Him.

People turned away from God and made wrong choices.

Those wrong choices separate us from God.

God had a plan to restore the relationship between Him and man.

God became a man named Jesus.

Jesus lived a perfect life.

He performed miracles and taught people about God.

He died on the cross to take the punishment for all of our wrong choices.

Three days later He rose from the dead.

After appearing to many, He returned to Heaven.

He promised to come back again. Those who believe in Him will spend enternity with Him.

Jesus' sacrifice and resurrection made a way for us to have a relationship with God once again.

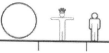

If you confess with your mouth that Jesus is Lord and believe in your heart that God raise Him from the dead, you will be saved. (Romans 10:9)

Anyone can have a friendship with God and receive the free gift of eternal life.

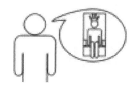

Chapter 9
Church History & Spiritual Warfare

Our God is the God of history. Our God is alive — and He works in time and space. His works are remembered in history. All of the books of the Old and New Testaments are historically accurate. Our entire faith comes from an event in history: the resurrection (*1 Corinthians 15:3-8*).

In the Old Testament, Israel was commanded to put memorials as stones of remembrance, so they would never forget the great works of God.

> *The people of Israel, under the leadership of Joshua, crossed into the Promised Land through the Jordan River. God miraculously opened a way for them through the river Jordan. As a reminder of God's miraculous act for them, He told Joshua to have them find 12 stones from the Jordan River and place them to remind the people and the following generations of how God provided a way for them. God expects us to remember what He has done for us. This is not just part of Israel's history but all who believe in God.* (See *Joshua 3:9-4:9*)

▶ **Question**: Every culture and people have a history about how they came to where they are today. Discuss the history of your people and culture. How did you come to the place you are today? God is a God of history — and we are called to remember.

1. We know God better by seeing how He has worked in the past. *Psalm 78:5-8* tells us to tell our children, and all following generations about the works of God, so they will more confidently put their trust in Him. We know what God is like by seeing what He has done in previous generations.

2. Church history covers doctrines and issues central to the faith. False teachers were common from the beginning (*Acts 20:29-31; 2 Tim. 3:1-9*). Paul and the other Apostles fought numerous doctrinal battles to maintain the purity of the faith. The same is true throughout church history.

3. Men and women have given their lives to defend the truths of the Word of God. And yet today, many attacks by false teachers continue. We can learn so much from how previous generations fought those battles and the conclusions they came to.

- We must know what battles have been fought. We must know what lessons have been learned. We must know what errors to avoid.

- We must honor those who have faithfully lived before us. *Hebrews 11* tells of those who lived by faith and did great things in faithful service for God. But the record did not end there. Many others have remained true to God and lived faithful lives.

- That is why biographies of great Christians are so encouraging to read. For example, Polycarp lived in the 2nd century and was the Christian bishop of Smyrna. He died a martyr, bound and burned at the stake, then stabbed when the fire failed to touch him. Before he died, he said these words: "Eighty-six years have I served Him, and He never did me any injury; how then can I blaspheme my King and my Savior. That is a legacy worth honoring!"

- Another example is Justin Martyr: In around AD 165 there was a man named Justin who was an early Christian theologian and defender of the faith. Justin and his five friends were brought before the governor for not worshiping and sacrificing to different gods. The governor said, "If you do not obey, you will be tortured without mercy." Justin responded, "That is our desire, to be tortured for Our Lord, Jesus Christ, and so to be saved, for that will give us salvation and firm confidence." And his friends joined in saying, "Do as you wish; for we are Christians, and we do not sacrifice to idols." The governor responded, "Those who do not wish to sacrifice to the gods and to obey the emperor will be scourged and beheaded according to the laws." Justin and his friends were beheaded for confessing their Savior.

- Another example: In AD 180 a woman named Donata was one of 12 Christians from the African country of Tunisia who were martyred. When called upon to sacrifice and worship Caesar, she replied, "We render to Caesar as Caesar, but worship and prayers to God alone." As a result, she and the others were beheaded.

▶ **Question**: What do you feel when you read these stories of Christians who gave up their life for their faith? If you have access to the internet you can go to: www.persecution.com for more stories like these.

Why Does Church History Matter?

- The story of Christianity impacts every believer in Jesus Christ. The history of the Christian faith affects how we read the Bible. It impacts how we view our government. It influences how we worship. Simply, the church's history is our family history. Past Christians are our mothers and fathers in the faith.

- When a child in your church asks, "How could Jesus be God and still be like me?" She is not asking a new question. She is dealing with an issue that, in AD 325, three hundred church leaders discussed in a little village named Nicaea, in the country of Turkey. Even if you've never heard of Nicaea, what those leaders decided will influence the way you answer the child's question. Read a version of the *Nicene Creed* below:

We believe in one God, the Father, the Almighty maker of Heaven and earth, of all that is seen and unseen. We believe in one Lord, Jesus Christ, the only Son of God, eternally begotten of the Father, God from God, Light from Light, true God from true God, begotten, not made, one in Being with the Father. Through him all things were made. For us and for our salvation he came down from Heaven by the power of the Holy Spirit, he was born of the Virgin Mary, and became man. For our sake he was crucified under Pontius Pilate; he suffered, died, and was buried. On the third day he rose again in fulfillment of the Scriptures; he ascended into Heaven and is seated at the right hand of the Father. He will come again in glory to judge the living and the dead, and His Kingdom will have no end. We believe in the Holy Spirit, the Lord, the giver of Life, who proceeds from the Father and the Son. With the Father and the Son he is worshiped and glorified. He has spoken through the Prophets. We believe in one holy universal and apostolic Church. We acknowledge one baptism…We look for the resurrection of the dead, and the life of the world to come. Amen.

Observation: Church history is very important. We have *"such a huge crowd of witnesses"* (*Heb. 12:1-2*), not only in the Bible, but also throughout the 2,000 years of the history of the church. Take a look at the following chart that summarizes the last 2,000 years of church history. As we finish this chapter, we want to remember the reality that we live in a spiritual world that is full of both godly and evil forces.

Name	Period	Characteristics
The Ancient Church	33-313 AD	Completion of the full Bible. Gospel spread from Jerusalem to Judea to the ends of the earth. Churches met in houses and various places. Persecution was everywhere!
Christian Empire	313-500 AD	Rome accepted Christianity as the official religion. The Church focused more on religion and rituals than true relationship with God. Political influence. Power and prestige.
Middle Ages	500-1500 AD	Islam grew rapidly and conquered. Catholic Church became most powerful and centralized. They taught salvation by works and ascetism (self-mortification for purity). Bible translated in people's languages in 1300's
Protestant Reformation (Start of the Protestant Church)	1500-1800 AD	Salvation is by grace through faith alone. Importance placed on accuracy of Bible doctrines. Great missionary movement, and the church spread across the world! The Great Awakening occurs.
Modern Era	1800-Today	Man's reasoning is above or equal with God. Everyone does what is right is his/her own mind. No one truth is superior to another. No absolutes. Modern and indigenous missionary movement spreads the Gospel to new/unreached areas.

Spiritual Warfare

There are two dangers when speaking and teaching about spiritual warfare.

- Some people go to one extreme by saying that demons are everywhere and are the cause of **everything** bad that happens.

- Others go to the other extreme and ignore the fact that we have an enemy (Satan and his demonic army) who hates God, and Christians and therefore they deny Satan's involvement in **anything**.

There are many examples of spiritual warfare in the Bible.

- Jesus recognized the difference between physical disease and spiritually demonic bondage. In *Matthew 4:24*, there were two types of people who were brought to Jesus for healing: those who were physically sick and those who were afflicted by demonic activity. *"People soon began bringing to him all who were sick. And whatever their sickness or disease, or if they were demon possessed or epileptic or paralyzed—he healed them all."* Jesus understood the difference and ministered to each group accordingly.

- Often mental disorders are simply physical in nature. They may be the result of chemical imbalances in the body, or the result of physical disease. Sometimes, however, they are spiritual in nature.

Consider this well-known encounter between Jesus and the man from Gerasenes as recorded by Luke, a medical doctor. Some considered this man demon possessed, while others thought he was a madman.

> So they arrived in the region of the Gerasenes, across the lake from Galilee. As Jesus was climbing out of the boat, a man who was possessed by demons came out to meet Him. For a long time He had been homeless and naked, living in a cemetery out-side the town. As soon as He saw Jesus, he shrieked and fell down in front of Him. Then he screamed, "Why are you interfering with me, Jesus, Son of the Most High God? Please, I beg you, don't torture me!" For Jesus had already commanded the evil spirit to come out of Him. This spirit had often taken control of the man. Even when he was placed under guard and put in chains and shackles, he simply broke them and rushed out into the wilderness, completely under the demon's power (Luke. 8:26-29).

<u>Observation</u>: This was a spiritual condition. Jesus recognized that in this case it was an issue of demon possession. Throughout the Bible, Satan and his demons were active in tempting, accusing, leading astray and destroying the works of God. One example is when Satan tempted Eve in the form of a serpent in the Garden of Eden as recorded in *Genesis 3:1-6*.

We live and minister in a world that has demonic beings working against us, and the things of the Lord. However, the Lord has given us His Holy Spirit and the Word of God to be victorious here on earth. He has already won our battle through the Resurrection of Jesus Christ. The same power that conquered the grave lives in us. We have been given the All Powerful, inspired Word of God and the person of the Holy Spirit. The Spirit controlled life of *Ephesians 5:15-21* gives us a lifestyle to live.

So be careful how you live. Don't live like fools, but like those who are wise. Make the most of every opportunity in these evil days. Don't act thoughtlessly, but understand what the Lord wants you to do. Don't be drunk with wine, because that will ruin your life. Instead, be filled with the Holy Spirit, singing psalms and hymns and spiritual songs among yourselves, and making music to the Lord in your hearts. And give thanks for everything to God the Father in the name of our Lord Jesus Christ. And further, submit to one another out of reverence for Christ.

Also, the Word filled life of *Colossians 3* equips us to live victoriously in Jesus no matter how much pain or difficulty we may go through. *Colossians 3:16-17* states:

> *Let the message about Christ, in all its richness, fill your lives. Teach and counsel each other with all the wisdom He gives. Sing psalms and hymns and spiritual songs to God with thankful hearts. And whatever you do or say, do it as a representative of the Lord Jesus, giving thanks through him to God the Father.*

▶ **Action Point**: Read *Ephesians 6:12-18*. Write down and draw a picture described as the armor of God.

A Portion of Church History (Joshua 3, 4)

God had a special place set aside for the Israelites to live.

The problem was there was a river preventing them from getting to it.

God parted the river so that they were able to cross.

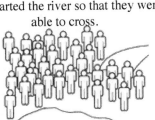

God told their leader to gather stones from the riverbed.

They built a monument there so generations could look back and remember what God did.

It was important for the Israelites to remember what God did.

It is also important for us to remember what God did throughout history, including Church History.

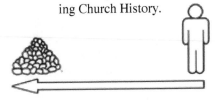

We can learn a lot about God by seeing how He worked in the past.

Your Investment

Congratulations! You have completed the written training for TTI Lite curriculum. By now you are a disciple who makes disciples. We pray you have started at least one or more multiplying churches that will impact your village, town, city and region for Jesus Christ.

You have invested a significant portion of your time, energy, gifts and focus to become a stronger follower of Jesus Christ and lead others with you for the sake of His Gospel. It is our honor to work in partnership with you and watch you grow as a disciple of Jesus Christ who starts churches for His glory.

One church that multiples many generations of churches eventually sees an orchard of churches in a region and country... in a continent and world... and we pray that is going to be you and your team.

You have gone through this book that helps you understand the art and science of interpreting God's Word. You have learned to communicate from the Word of God with passion, clarity and accuracy. You have used a practical work on starting a new church and church planting center from the Book of *Acts*. You have studied the treasure of the Old Testament.

Friends, you have looked at the life of Jesus, our Savior and Lord from all Four Gospels, combined together in a mixture that can only cause us to worship Him, love Him and fear Him. You have been motivated by Paul, in his writings for us to live life in the church with Truth. The rest of the New Testament was covered in a way that gave freshness from each book to our daily lives for godliness in the Spirit.

You examined essential doctrines to help you know what you believe and why you teach these Truths. Finally, you completed this book with why you believe in Jesus as the Perfect God and Man. You read about the activity of God throughout the history of the Church and the ongoing reality of our enemy: the world, the flesh and Satan; we have won through Christ Jesus and the battle still rages.

You have received well-rounded training. God now calls you to multiply even more what you have learned and invest your life; investing in others by making disciples who make disciples. You make disciples by going, by reaching out to those without Jesus Christ as their personal

Savior and God, winning them to Christ under the power of the Holy Spirit and then baptizing them. At that point their new life starts by you and others teaching them all that Jesus commanded in His Word (*Matthew 28:18-20*). That will take a lifetime... a lifetime where He will be with you always.

Let's worship the King whom this Book is dedicated to, the King of kings, Jesus Christ. In Heaven we will be together for the parade of nations at His throne. We look forward to being there with you to celebrate His name, His activity and His power. We will smile and rejoice in the Spirit when we see so many that will come into His Kingdom because of His grace through you and your church planting church, a center of Kingdom influence. We are proud of you. We love you! Our arms are locked with yours. We are on His marching orders. Until we all meet on this day:

> *After this I saw a vast crowd, too great to count, from every nation and tribe and people and language, standing in front of the throne and before the Lamb. They were clothed in white robes and held palm branches in their hands. And they were shouting with a great roar, "Salvation comes from our God who sits on the throne and from the Lamb!" And all the angels were standing around the throne and around the elders and the four living beings. And they fell before the throne with their faces to the ground and worshiped God. They sang, "Amen! Blessing and glory and wisdom and thanksgiving and honor and power and strength belong to our God forever and ever! Amen." (Rev. 7:9-12)*

Charts and Illustrations

Examples of Multiplication/Reproduction

It is recommend that each church planter create a chart similar to the ones on this page for each church they plant. This will help you accurately monitor and assess the success of TTI students when it comes to seeing churches planted, reproduced, and multiplied.

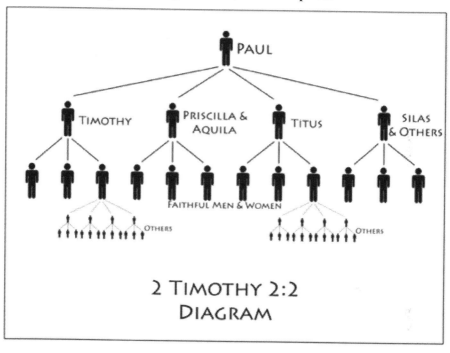

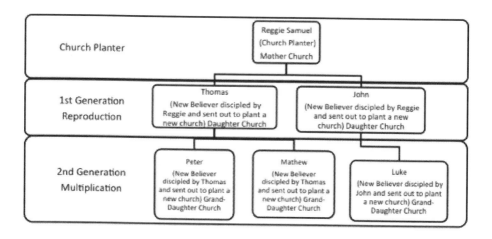

What is the Bible?

Answer: It is God's Word, written down. It is the way that He communicates with us.

How did we get the Bible?

Answer: *Inspiration*

The words in the Bible are God breathed…they are completely accurate and free from error.

God's Breath ⟶ **Writers** = **Bible**

How was the Bible transmitted?

The Bible was communicated orally… and historically written down and reproduced.

Translation:

Original Language into a local language.

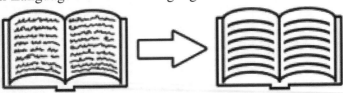

Importance of Application:

You must apply what you've learned. Consider *Luke 10:25-37* as you have already studied this above using the SWORD method.

A Jewish man was attacked by robbers.

Several Jewish religious men passed by, but they offered no help.

An outsider (Samaritan) rescued and cared for the man.

Which of these men was a neighbor to the man who was attacked?

The outsider (Samaritan)

Jesus told them, "Go and do likewise."

Possible applications:

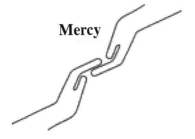

Mercy

Love others as yourself

**Love through actions,
not only words**

Do not show prejudice

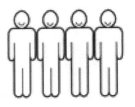

Communicating the Word of God

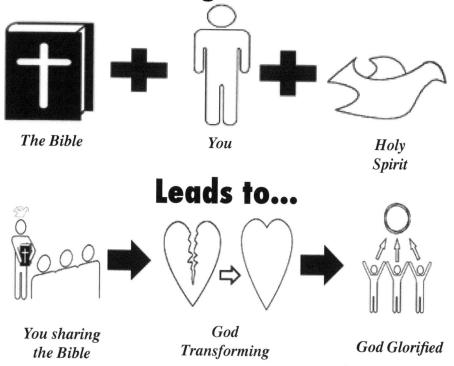

The Bible   *You*   *Holy Spirit*

Leads to...

You sharing the Bible   *God Transforming*   *God Glorified*

The Role of the Holy Spirit in Communicating the Bible

For the speaker the Holy Spirit provides:

1. Understanding of God's truth and the Bible
2. Guidance
3. Empowerment

For the listener the Holy Spirit provides:

1. Conviction
2. Transformation

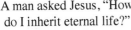

Communicating: When having a conversation, there are several things to remember. Observe how Jesus told this story:

The Story	Jesus	You
A man asked Jesus, "How do I inherit eternal life?"	Answered & asked questions: "What does the law say?"	Engage your audience. Ask and take questions. Choose relevant topics.

Man asks for clarification: Law says love God and neighbor. Who is my neighbor?	Answers with a story: A man was robbed and left for dead. Two men ignored him, and one helped.	Use stories to help them understand.

The man understands the story: The man who helped was the neighbor.	Tells him to go and do likewise	Give a call of action to obedience and an application

  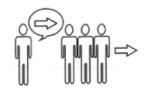

As you communicate the Word of God to others, encourage others to do the same also.

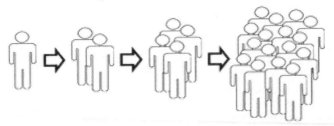

The Great Commission & Church Planting

We are empowered (*Acts 1:8*)

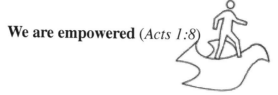

We are sent (*John 20:21*)

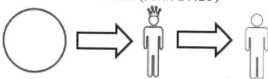

 To everyone, everywhere (*Mark 16:15*)

With a strategy (*Matthew 28:18-20*)

 **Telling a message — the Gospel** (*Luke 24:44-49*)

Equipped and filled for the task (*Acts 1:8*)

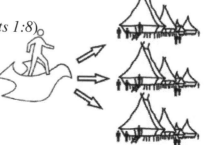

Summary of the Old Testament

The Law
Genesis through
Deuteronomy:
All nations will be
blessed through
you.

God tells Abraham
he will have a
son, even though
Abraham
and his wife are
old.

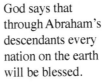

God says that
through Abraham's
descendants every
nation on the earth
will be blessed.

Jesus is a descen-
dent of Abraham.
He is the blessing
to all nations.

History Books
One example:
Ruth — Kinsman
Redeemer

Ruth's husband
dies

Someone from
her husband's line
redeems her and
marries her, taking
Ruth
under his
protec-
tion.

Similarly, Jesus
is our Kinsman
Redeemer.

Poetry Books:
*"They divide my
garments among
themselves and
throw dice for my
clothing."*
(Psalms 22:18)

*"They divide my
garments among
themselves..."*

*... and throw dice
for my clothing."*

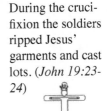

During the cruci-
fixion the soldiers
ripped Jesus'
garments and cast
lots. *(John 19:23-
24)*

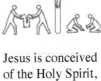

Prophets:
*"The Lord himself
will give you
the sign. Look!
The virgin will
conceive a child!
She will give birth
to a son and will
call him Imman-
uel (which means
'God with us.')"*
(Psalms 22:18)

*"The Lord himself
will give you the
sign. Look! The
virgin will con-
ceive a child!"*

*"She will give
birth to a son and
will call him
Immanuel."*

Jesus is conceived
of the Holy Spirit,
born of the virgin
Mary. *(Matthew
1:18)*

Summary of the Life of Jesus

An angel told Mary that, by the Power of the Holy Spirit, she would conceive a son.

She would name Him Jesus, and He would be the Son of God.

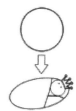

When Jesus grew up, He started His ministry.

He was baptized.

He called disciples to join Him.

He performed miracles like healing the sick.

Raising the dead...

He taught people about His Father.

It seemed like everyone loved Jesus...

But some people did not. They wanted Jesus to die.

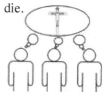

They falsely accused Him.

He was crucified, and He died.

He was buried.

After three days He rose from the dead!

He appeared to His disciples and many others.

He told His disciples to tell everyone His story.

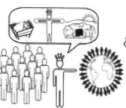

He ascended into Heaven.

He will return to take those who believe to be with Him.

Luke 15:11-32

A man had two sons.

One son asked for his inheritance early.

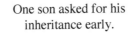

He wasted it.

He was left in poverty.

He decided to return home.

His father was waiting for him.

The father ran to him.

He gave him new clothes and had a celebration.

His oldest son was mad at His father's response.

God is:

Love

Grace

Forgiveness

Restoration

Teaches us about man's...

Sinfulness

Rebellion

Repentance

Pride

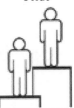

John 4:1-42

There were two groups of people who did not like each other:
the Jews and the Samaritans.

Jesus was traveling through Samaria.

He was tired, and he asked a woman for a drink.

She was confused because Jews did not talk to Samaritans.

Jesus says He gives water that will make her never thirst again.

She asks for that water.

Jesus asks her to call for her husband.

She says she has no husband.

Jesus says that she has had five husbands, and the man she is with now is not her husband.

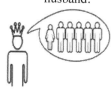

Jesus reveals Himself as Messiah.

The woman is amazed by what He knew and tells her village. Many believe and follow Jesus.

We are Not Just "Hearers" of the Word, but "Doers" (James 1:22)

We are doers of God's Word, not just hearers.

Like a man that built his house upon a rock:

The rains came...

The house stood firm.

Whoever hears and does not do what God says

Is like a man that built his house upon the sand:

The rains came...

The house fell.

Major Bible Doctrines Summarized in Picture Form

I believe in God, the Father Almighty

Creator of heaven and earth

I believe in Jesus Christ, His only Son, our Lord

Who was conceived by the Holy Spirit

Born of the Virgin Mary

Suffered under Pontius Pilate

Was crucified, died

And was buried

On the third day He rose again from the dead

He ascended into heaven

And is seated at the right hand of God the Father Almighty

From there He will come to judge the living and the dead

I believe in the Holy Spirit

The Universal Church

The Communion of the Saints

The forgiveness of sins

The resurrection of the body

And the life everlasting - Amen

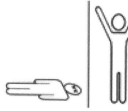

Story to Share When Defending Your Faith

In the beginning there was God.

He created the heavens and the earth.

He created people to have friendship with Him.

People turned away from God and made wrong choices.

Those wrong choices separate us from God.

God had a plan to restore the relationship between Him and man.

God became a man named Jesus.

Jesus lived a perfect life.

He performed miracles and taught people about God.

He died on the cross to take the punishment for all of our wrong choices.

Three days later He rose from the dead.

After appearing to many, He returned to Heaven.

He promised to come back again. Those who believe in Him will spend enternity with Him.

Jesus' sacrifice and resurrection made a way for us to have a relationship with God once again.

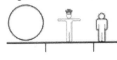

If you confess with your mouth that Jesus is Lord and believe in your heart that God raise Him from the dead, you will be saved. (Romans 10:9)

Anyone can have a friendship with God and receive the free gift of eternal life.

A Portion of Church History (Joshua 3, 4)

God had a special place set aside for the Israelites to live.

The problem was there was a river preventing them from getting to it.

God parted the river so that they were able to cross.

God told their leader to gather stones from the riverbed.

They built a monument there so generations could look back and remember what God did.

It was important for the Israelites to remember what God did.

It is also important for us to remember what God did throughout history, including Church History.

We can learn a lot about God by seeing how He worked in the past.

Bible Reading Guide

Old Testament Reading Guide:

Every day, listen or read one chapter from the Old Testament. You will complete the full Old Testament in three years because it has 929 chapters. Each chapter you read, cross out the corresponding number for that chapter.

New Testament Reading Guide:

Every day, listen or read one chapter from the New Testament. You will complete the full New Testament in only 260 days because it has only 260 chapters. Each chapter you read, cross out the corresponding number for that chapter.

Genesis 1 2 3 4 5 6 7 8 9 10 11 12 13 14 15 16 17 18 19 20 21 22 23 24 25 26 27 28 29 30 31 32 33 34 35 36 37 38 39 40 41 42 43 44 45 46 47 48 49 50

Exodus 1 2 3 4 5 6 7 8 9 10 11 12 13 14 15 16 17 18 19 20 21 22 23 24 25 26 27 28 29 30 31 32 33 34 35 36 37 38 39 40

Leviticus 1 2 3 4 5 6 7 8 9 10 11 12 13 14 15 16 17 18 19 20 21 22 23 24 25 26 27

Numbers 1 2 3 4 5 6 7 8 9 10 11 12 13 14 15 16 17 18 19 20 21 22 23 24 25 26 27 28 29 30 31 32 33 34 35 36

Deuteronomy 1 2 3 4 5 6 7 8 9 10 11 12 13 14 15 16 17 18 19 20 21 22 23 24 25 26 27 28 29 30 31 32 33 34

Joshua 1 2 3 4 5 6 7 8 9 10 11 12 13 14 15 16 17 18 19 20 21 22 23 24

Judges 1 2 3 4 5 6 7 8 9 10 11 12 13 14 15 16 17 18 19 20 21

Ruth 1 2 3 4

1 Samuel 1 2 3 4 5 6 7 8 9 10 11 12 13 14 15 16 17 18 19 20 21 22 23 24 25 26 27 28 29 30 31

2 Samuel 1 2 3 4 5 6 7 8 9 10 11 12 13 14 15 16 17 18 19 20 21 22 23 24

1 Kings 1 2 3 4 5 6 7 8 9 10 11 12 13 14 15 16 17 18 19 20 21 22

2 Kings 1 2 3 4 5 6 7 8 9 10 11 12 13 14 15 16 17 18 19 20 21 22 23 24 25

1 Chronicles 1 2 3 4 5 6 7 8 9 10 11 12 13 14 15 16 17 18 19 20 21 22 23 24 25 26 27 28 29

2 Chronicles 1 2 3 4 5 6 7 8 9 10 11 12 13 14 15 16 17 18 19 20 21 22 23 24 25 26 27 28 29 30 31 32 33 34 35 36

Ezra 1 2 3 4 5 6 7 8 9 10

Nehemiah 1 2 3 4 5 6 7 8 9 10 11 12 13

Esther 1 2 3 4 5 6 7 8 9 10

Job 1 2 3 4 5 6 7 8 9 10 11 12 13 14 15 16 17 18 19 20 21 22 23 24 25 26 27 28 29 30 31 32 33 34 35 36 37 38 39 40 41 42

Psalms 1 2 3 4 5 6 7 8 9 10 11 12 13 14 15 16 17 18 19 20 21 22 23 24 25 26 27 28 29 30 31 32 33 34 35 36 37 38 39 40 41 42 43 44 45 46 47 48 49 50 51 52 53 54 55 56 57 58 59 60 61 62 63 64 65 66 67 68 69 70 71 72 73 74 75 76 77 78 79 80 81 82 83 84 85 86 87 88 89 90 91 92 93 94 95 96 97 98 99 100 101 102 103 104 105 106 107 108 109 110 111 112 113 114 115 116 117 118 119 120 121 122 123 124 125 126 127 128 129 130 131 132 133 134 135 136 137 138 139 140 141 142 143 144 145 146 147 148 149 150

Proverbs 1 2 3 4 5 6 7 8 9 10 11 12 13 14 15 16 17 18 19 20 21 22 23 24 25 26 27 28 29 30 31

Ecclesiastes 1 2 3 4 5 6 7 8 9 10 11 12

Song of Songs 1 2 3 4 5 6 7 8

Isaiah 1 2 3 4 5 6 7 8 9 10 11 12 13 14 15 16 17 18 19 20 21 22 23 24 25 26 27 28 29 30 31 32 33 34 35 36 37 38 39 40 41 42 43 44 45 46 47 48 49 50 51 52 53 54 55 56 57 58 59 60

Jeremiah 1 2 3 4 5 6 7 8 9 10 11 12 13 14 15 16 17 18 19 20 21 22 23 24 25 26 27 28 29 30 31 32 33 34 35 36 37 38 39 40 41 42 43 44 45 46 47 48 49 50 51 52

Lamentations 1 2 3 4 5

Ezekiel 1 2 3 4 5 6 7 8 9 10 11 12 13 14 15 16 17 18 19 20 21 22 23 24 25 26 27 28 29 30 31 32 33 34 35 36 37 38 39 40 41 42 43 44 45 46 47 48

Daniel 1 2 3 4 5 6 7 8 9 10 11 12

Hosea 1 2 3 4 5 6 7 8 9 10 11 12 13 14

Joel 1 2 3

Old Testament Reading Guide

Amos	1 2 3 4 5 6 7 8 9
Obadiah	1
Jonah	1 2 3 4
Micah	1 2 3 4 5 6 7
Nahum	1 2 3
Habbakuk	1 2 3
Zephaniah	1 2 3
Haggai	1 2
Zechariah	1 2 3 4 5 6 7 8 9 10 11 12 13 14
Malachi	1 2 3 4

Book	Chapters
Matthew	1 2 3 4 5 6 7 8 9 10 11 12 13 14 15 16 17 18 19 20 21 22 23 24 25 26 27 28
Mark	1 2 3 4 5 6 7 8 9 10 11 12 13 14 15 16
Luke	1 2 3 4 5 6 7 8 9 10 11 12 13 14 15 16 17 18 19 20 21 22 23 24
John	1 2 3 4 5 6 7 8 9 10 11 12 13 14 15 16 17 18 19 20 21
Acts	1 2 3 4 5 6 7 8 9 10 11 12 13 14 15 16 17 18 19 20 21 22 23 24 25 26 27 28
Romans	1 2 3 4 5 6 7 8 9 10 11 12 13 14 15 16
1 Corinthians	1 2 3 4 5 6 7 8 9 10 11 12 13 14 15 16
2 Corinthians	1 2 3 4 5 6 7 8 9 10 11 12 13
Galatians	1 2 3 4 5 6
Ephesians	1 2 3 4 5 6
Philippians	1 2 3 4
Colossians	1 2 3 4 5
1 Thessalonians	1 2 3 4 5
2 Thessalonians	1 2 3
1 Timothy	1 2 3 4 5 6
2 Timothy	1 2 3 4

Titus	1	2	3																		
Philemon	1																				
Hebrews	1	2	3	4	5	6	7	8	9	10	11	12	13								
James	1	2	3	4	5																
1 Peter	1	2	3	4	5																
2 Peter	1	2	3																		
1 John	1	2	3	4	5	6	7	8	9	10	11	12	13	14	15	16					
2 John	1																				
3 John	1																				
Jude	1																				
Revelation	1	2	3	4	5	6	7	8	9	10	11	12	13	14	15	16	17	18	19	20	21 22

Made in the USA
Charleston, SC
19 May 2015